Commercials on Compact Disc

Advertiser	Commercial Name
1. Chevrolet Camaro:	Yes, Yes, Yes
2. AT&T:	Everything You Taught Me
3. RisCassi & Davis Law Firm:	Why Advertise?
4. Lo Jack Stolen Vehicle Recovery System:	Nick Bell
5. KNBC TV:	I Bought a Gun
6. Thieves Market:	Closet
7. Thieves Market:	Sale that Cried Wolf
8. Thieves Market:	Strike
9. Thieves Market:	Herb
10. L.A. Gear:	Adventures of a Single Girl
11. L.A. Gear:	Diary of a Single Girl
12. Alpine Car Stereos:	Clapton
13. P.E.I. Potatoes:	CODCO
14. Listerine:	Polka
15. Dixie Value Mall:	Professor
16. Freixenet:	Refrigeratorologist
17. Freixenet:	Pronunciation
18. Freixenet:	Another Name
19. Freixenet:	How to Crash a Party
20. Sting:	Something New
21. Molson:	Comedy
22. Molson:	Notice
23. Molson:	Designated Driver
24. Molson:	Border
25. Fromageries Bel Cheese:	Craving
26. Fromageries Bel Cheese:	Valley Girl 1

Effective
Radio
Advertising

Effective Radio Advertising

Marc G. Weinberger
Leland Campbell
Beth Brody

LEXINGTON BOOKS
An Imprint of Macmillan, Inc.
NEW YORK

Maxwell Macmillan Canada
TORONTO

Maxwell Macmillan International
NEW YORK   OXFORD   SINGAPORE   SYDNEY

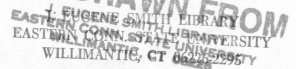

Library of Congress Cataloging-in-Publication Data

Weinberger, Marc G.
  Effective radio advertising / Marc G. Weinberger, Leland Campbell,
Beth Brody.
    p. cm.
  ISBN 0-669-25003-1
  1. Radio advertising—United States. I. Campbell, Leland.
II. Brody, Beth. III. Title.
HF6146.R3W43 1994
659. 14'2—dc20   94-25058
                                                          CIP

Lexington Books
An Imprint of Macmillan, Inc.
866 Third Avenue, New York, N. Y. 10022

Maxwell Macmillan Canada, Inc.
1200 Eglinton Avenue East
Suite 200
Don Mills, Ontario M3C 3N1

Macmillan, Inc. is part of the Maxwell Communication
Group of Companies.

Printed in the United States of America

printing number
1 2 3 4 5 6 7 8 9 10

Contents

Foreword   v
Preface   vii

1   Radio: Its Golden Past and Glowing Future   1

2   Radio: A Uniquely Powerful Medium   15

3   Putting Radio in Your Plan   37

4   Getting Specific: Finding Patterns in the Sand   61

5   Anatomy of a Good Commercial
for High-Risk Tools—WHITE Cell Products   81

6   Anatomy of a Good Commercial
for High-Risk Toys—RED Cell Products   101

7   Anatomy of a Good Commercial
for Low-Risk Tools—BLUE Cell Products   113

8   Anatomy of a Good Commercial
for Low-Risk Treats—YELLOW Cell Products   127

9   Epilogue   143

Appendix A   Radio Recall Research, Inc. Method
and Response Measures   147
Appendix B   Coded Commercial Features Used   151
Appendix C   Correlations Among Measures   155
Appendix D   Classification Rates from Discriminant Analysis   157

References   161
Index   167
About the Authors   175

Foreword

During the more than forty years that I've been selling radio advertising, I've watched it develop into a versatile and sophisticated advertising medium. Today, each radio station has its own unique personality that can make advertisers' cash registers sing and agency creatives win highly esteemed awards. Radio is the medium that is with us when we wake up in the morning, go for a jog, commute to and from our jobs, work at our desks, and cook our evening meals. In fact, the average radio listener spends nearly three-and-a-half hours each weekday and five hours each weekend listening to the radio.

Yet despite radio's effectiveness and popularity, this powerful medium is still underutilized by much of the advertising community.

I believe that *Effective Radio Advertising* will greatly benefit the radio advertising community because it demonstrates through well-thought-out and documented research what makes successful, effective radio commercials. With targeted, creative radio copy, advertisers and their agencies can rise above the din to communicate effectively with their audience. Radio has always been the medium that gets the best results for its advertisers. Because of its unique ability to reach the right listeners with the right message, radio even survived the onslaught of television and cable. But for radio to continue to expand and to continue to effectively reach consumers, we must always be searching for new, creative ways to advertise products on radio. I welcome this book because the creative concepts discussed throughout are vital to the continued success of radio advertising.

For advertising agencies and their client advertisers to truly understand the meaning of radio, they must start at the beginning–with clear creative concepts that can be turned into masterpieces of sound. This book details how an advertiser can create both successful ads and successful campaigns. In the same way that long-standing, award-winning campaigns such as those for Molson Ale or Laughing Cow Cheeses have helped to promote excellence in radio creativity and caused agencies and advertisers to take more notice of radio, this book will help our industry take a fresh look at itself and become much stronger in the process.

Whether you are trying to win a client with an exciting new idea, affect the behavior of a target group of heavy users of a product, or search for the best way to send a message to a market, radio can't be overlooked. This book will help make the message more effective, *Effective Radio Advertising* offers our industry the tools to be more creative, more effective, and more successful.

Ralph Guild
Chairman
The Interep Radio Store

Preface

We were inspired to write this book because we were struck by the marginal or non-existent role of radio in the media mixes of most large advertisers—a fact that is out of all proportion with the potential benefits of radio. This neglect of radio by advertisers arises in part from the lack of research and understanding of radio's potentially powerful roles in a total advertising campaign. When we began the research to write this book, we were stunned to find how little prior research had been conducted and how little was written about radio advertising. This book is designed to help change the negative perceptions that exist within the advertising community about radio's role in the media mix by filling in the information void and clearly demonstrating how radio is an extremely powerful, yet often underutilized, advertising medium.

Media supervisors, planners, and buyers at both advertising agencies and client advertiser companies will find that this book challenges them to consider using radio by offering clear-cut research that demonstrates the effectiveness of the medium. Those at agencies or radio stations developing creative strategies and writing ads will find the prescriptions for successful ads an important input to their daily work. And, of course, those teaching media planning and the creative aspects of advertising and those studying advertising in college or in seminars will want to consult this work to discover how radio can be used effectively.

The book relies on an extensive use of radio success stories as well as research into the factors that make radio ads tick and make money for advertisers. The clear conclusion is that radio has an important part to play in the media mix either as a leading actor or in a highly supportive role.

The first part of the book highlights the value of radio and focuses on how radio can easily be incorporated into an effective media plan. Radio's flexibility and targeting strengths suggest that the absence of radio in a media mix should be the extreme exception, not the norm.

The second half of the book describes what elements constitute effective ("good") and non-effective ("bad") radio ads. Good and bad ads leave very different fingerprints embedded in the Message Style, Structure, and Presenter features of the ads' creative elements. The results provide those developing radio advertising with a road map of what message tactics do and do not work well for various product categories. These prescriptions are not based on the authors' subjective opinions, but result from a comprehensive analysis of more than 2,000 radio ads pretested by a leading research company, Radio Recall Research, Inc. Furthermore, by basing this work on product types and by examining a large base of ads that show what has worked and failed in the past, we provide clear evidence about appropriate Message Structure, Style, and Presenter features that add or detract from an ad.

A writing and research project of this size requires much more than the effort of three people. This book represents the cooperative involvement of a large number of individuals and organizations. To start, we are particularly indebted to Radio Recall Research, Inc. for their patience and trust in our efforts, and especially to Ted Brew. Their data files of more than 2,000 ads provided us with the raw materials to develop the analysis of the radio ads. Without their generosity, there would not have been a book.

We owe a note of appreciation to the School of Management

at the University of Massachusetts for its research support. We are also indebted to Sue Latremouille of the Radio Marketing Bureau in Canada; Jodi Mutnansky, Laura Morandin, and Ken Costa of the Radio Advertising Bureau in New York; and Ralph Guild of The Interep Radio Store, all for being patient with our repeated phone calls and answering our lengthy questions.

Finally, we owe a large debt to our families for believing that this five-year effort that took precious time away from them would be successful. Thank you Sharon, Michelle, and Danny Weinberger; Roni Campbell; and Russell Brody. It is to all of you that we dedicate this work.

Effective
Radio
Advertising

Chapter 1

Radio: Its Golden Past and Glowing Future

The wiseman knows that the very polestar of prudence lies in steering by the wind.

—Balasar Gracian

R adio is a unique, growing, and pervasive medium. Unique in its ability to deliver electronic advertising messages to well-defined geographic and demographically selective audiences. Growing to the point where, today, there are nearly 10,000 commercial AM and FM radio stations in the United States and more than 700 in Canada. Pervasive because it is a medium, like no other, that is routinely found in virtually every room in our homes, in our offices, in our vehicles, and in the places where we relax. The omnipresence of radio provides tremendous opportunities for advertisers. Radio offers a greater capacity for delivering advertising messages—to any number of highly targeted demographic audiences—than has been recognized by the advertising community.

Though radio has tremendous potential to effectively reach and influence consumers, it is greatly underutilized by most companies, particularly larger advertisers. As the following pages demonstrate, there is tremendous impact to be gained by moving larger shares of media budgets into radio and by learning to develop more effective radio messages.

The Early Days of Radio

Before examining the strategic and tactical uses of radio, it's helpful to take a look at radio's history and its role in advertising. The introduction of radio in the early 1900s coincided with historical and economic events, providing technology that helped bring about important worldwide changes. At the turn of the century, trade and travel by ship around the globe was developing at an increasing rate. The concept of world war was about to become a stark reality, and a revolution in production technology was emerging. Retailing, fueled by urban growth, was moving to mass distribution through the expansion of large department stores soon to be followed by modern grocery chain stores. The telephone was still an invention that was not widely available and only allowed one-on-one communication over cables. The horse and buggy was about to make way for the automobile. The increasingly mobile world and the developing industrial giants would need more—and better—communication to fuel further progress.

Wireless Communication Enters the Picture

The need to reliably communicate was answered by Guglielmo Marconi's invention of the wireless telegraphy. Ironically, it was a wireless operator during the Titanic disaster of 1912, young David Sarnoff, who would fully comprehend the future of wireless communication. Sarnoff knew firsthand the power of wireless technology, and by 1916 he was advocating the wireless as a household utility that could receive music, lectures, and baseball scores. He suggested that radio stations be supported by the sale of radios and that those who owned stations would gain great goodwill and recognition by having their names repeated over the air. Westinghouse, one of the early companies to own a radio station, indeed gained goodwill and sold radio receivers as Sarnoff predicted, but there were many others on the sidelines who were to see the tremendous advantages of having their names repeated over the air.

The Birth of Mass Communication

With mass production techniques being developed by Henry Ford and other industrial magnates, and with mass distribution networks emerging, there was a growing need to stimulate consumer demand at a rate to keep goods moving from factories to retail stores to consumers. For the industrial wheel to keep turning, mass consumption had to match mass production. The obvious way to accomplish this was through mass communication. Radio arrived at just the right moment in history to help fuel this basic economic need. Frank Conrad, founder of KDKA in Pittsburgh, discovered that he could exchange publicity to the local Hamilton Music Store for phonograph records to help him fill radio air time. Westinghouse bought KDKA and other stations when they realized that more and better radio programs also fueled demand for their radio receiving sets.

Not-so-Subtle Messages

Within a decade of Sarnoff's predictions, hundreds of radio stations had been created, major radio networks were established, and advertising was the accepted method of funding the medium. WEAF in New York, a station then owned by another giant of the electronic industry, AT&T, ran the first U.S. radio commercial in 1922—a ten-minute infomercial for apartments in Hawthorne Park in Jackson Heights, Queens. This first ad cost $50 and attracted other advertisers such as Gimbel's department stores, Tidewater Oil, and the American Express Company.

The norm in the early years was the sponsorship of a program with very little mention of the product—much akin to the sponsorship today on public television in the United States of "Masterpiece Theater" by the Mobil Corporation. An advertiser like Gillette could be a bit more direct and develop programming that discussed fashion in facial hair and cleanliness and, not coincidentally, modern safety razors. More typical of the early 1920s were simple sponsorships in which the name of the advertiser was associated with the programming much in the same manner of today's sporting events like the Sunkist Citrus Bowl or Virginia Slims Tour. Back in the 1920s a radio listener could tune into the American Tobacco Company's "Lucky Strike Radio Show," the Maxwell House "Showboat." Ipana "Troubadours," and a lengthy list of other corporate sponsors all treading on the fringes of modern radio advertising.

However, this unobtrusive form of promotion was not entirely voluntary. Some stations such as AT&T's WEAF imposed strict guidelines that prohibited "plugs": the mention of price, size, and shape of package as well as the distribution of sample merchandise. By 1926 there were many competing radio stations that did not impose these same restrictions on advertisers, and the floodgates for advertising messages, rather than sponsorships, flung open. Between 1927 and 1930 the dollars spent on advertising messages soared from $4 million to $40 million, and with it came the beginning of the direct-sell ad.

The Big Three Networks

Network radio developed with AT&T's transmission technology and ownership of WEAF in New York. With its efficient means of cable transmission of sound, AT&T linked up twenty-three stations from Boston to California into a chain broadcasting organization that set the pattern for today's radio network system. To avoid losing its telephone monopoly, AT&T was forced to sell its network to a new subsidiary of RCA, the National Broadcasting Corporation, controlled by the visionary David Sarnoff. The acquired network became the NBC Red Network and the old RCA-owned stations became the NBC Blue Network. The NBC Red Network, fed from WEAF (later WNBC and WFAN), carried many of the programs that had been with AT&T and garnered most of the advertising dollars. The NBC Blue Network, also based in New York (WJZ), focused on public affairs and cultural programming. Later, in 1927 a third U.S. national network, to become known as the Columbia Broadcasting System, was started in Philadelphia.

Though advertising on the three networks was still largely program sponsorship, local stations welcomed spot announcements as an attractive revenue source for both network affiliated and unaffiliated stations which could be inserted during station breaks from network programming feeds.

Establishing Codes of Ethics

As commercials became more common and intrusive, the National Association of Broadcasters (NAB) in the United States and the Canadian Association of Broadcasting (CAB) established a code of ethics that sought to gain voluntary compliance among radio stations to regulate advertising by reserving the daytime hours for hard-sell ads and the evening hours for the more institutional-style sponsorships. However, the depression brought the need for stations and networks to hold and attract more advertisers, so by the early 1930s many of the old network taboos against mentioning price were abandoned and hard-sell ads became common. In 1931 A&P Food Stores became the first network advertiser to break the ban against mentioning product features.[1]

Radio's Rapid Growth

Through the years, radio, with its invisible waves, remained a vehicle with almost mystical power to entertain and inform audiences and to link producers and potential consumers. The rapid growth of radio advertising revenues mirrored the explosion of radio entering U.S. homes. By 1940 90% of homes had a radio. It was an advertiser's dream! In 1930 ad revenues were over $40 million, by 1940 they increased nearly fourfold to over $150 million, and by the end of the war in 1945 revenues had doubled to over $300 million.

From fewer than 1,000 AM stations on air during the war, there were over 2,000 stations by 1950, and over 4,000 by 1965. This growth, together with the rise of FM radio from 68 stations in 1945 to nearly 5,000 in 1994, provides advertisers with a tremendous opportunity for segmentation and targeting because there is a greater variety in programming formats for listeners. For example, by simply choosing the correct radio format and daypart, advertisers today can narrowly pinpoint and reach a male radio listener between the ages of eighteen and twenty-five, females aged thirty-five to fifty-four, or senior citizens over sixty. Chapter 2 goes into greater detail about radio's unique targeting ability.

Television Enters the Picture

When commercial television in the United States stepped into the limelight in the 1950s, there were just 2,612 radio stations on the air, and radio ad revenue actually dropped in the midst of a booming national economy. However, since TV fully came to prominence, the number of radio stations has increased nearly fourfold. Radio is surely alive and well, but the appealingly large network television audiences caused many large advertisers to place their advertising dollars into television. Today in the United States radio represents less than 7% of all advertising spending (see Table 1–1). The gild never went off radio's advertising lily, but it has been overshadowed by a dependency that many ad agencies and advertisers have with the mass market audiences of television.

The Structure of Radio

The average radio listener may notice the difference between a locally produced ad and a nationally produced ad, but most listeners are oblivious to the distinction between local spot, national spot, wired network, or unwired network commercials. Local spot radio advertising—advertising placed directly with a local station by a local advertiser or its local ad agency—accounts for over three-quarters of total radio spending. But larger regional and national advertisers with broader product distribution often require the ease and breadth of network buys,

Table 1–1
Percent Share of Advertising Revenues by Media, U.S. and Canada

	U.S. 1950 (%)	U.S. 1955 (%)	U.S. 1970 (%)	U.S. 1993 (%)	Canada 1976 (%)	Canada 1980 (%)	Canada 1985 (%)	Canada 1992 (%)
Newspaper Total	36.3	33.6	29.2	23.1	35.5	32.5	30.2	27.6
National	9.1	9.8	4.6	2.6				
Local	27.2	25.9	24.6	20.5				
Magazines	8.4	7.6	6.6	5.4	3	4.4	3.4	3
Television Total	3	11.3	18.4	22.2	14.4	16.2	16.7	19.4
Radio Total	10.6	5	6.7	6.8	10.8	10.4	9	8.3
Outdoor	2.5	2.1	1.2	0.7	6.8	6.4	7.5	8.5
Miscellaneous (including direct mail, business papers, and others)	38.2	38.8	37.6	41.9	29.5	30.1	33.2	33.2

Source: Statistics Canada and *Advertising Age*, April 30, 1980; February 16, 1981; May 4, 1992; January 4, 1993; September 29, 1993. (1993 estimates derived from figures of Robert J. Coen, McCann-Erickson.)

unwired network buys, or the flexibility of spot market radio purchases.

National Spot Radio

National spot radio is customarily placed through national station representative firms—such as The Interep Radio Store, Katz Radio Group, or CBS Radio Representatives—which represent the interests of radio stations to advertising agencies and national advertisers for national advertising time placement. In essence, each national radio rep firm acts as sales agent or broker between the agency and radio station in the buying and selling of national advertising time.

The definition of a spot purchase versus a local market buy can get confusing when the local offices of a national ad agency place ads directly with stations in their home cities for a national advertiser rather than buy through national radio rep firms. The agency saves the radio rep commission but it confuses the label "local radio" a bit. In other words, local radio means more than just local, retail advertisers: it can simply mean an ad for a national advertiser placed through the local office of a national ad agency.

Wired Networks

The radio networks have undergone substantial change since their formation in the 1920s. The term "wired" networks is a holdover from the days of AT&T's transmission cables that linked its affiliated stations to simultaneously broadcast the same program. Today most of the wired networks involve stations under contract but not owned by the network, and the transmissions are received by satellite, not cable wires. For the advertiser or agency, the wired network buy avoids the tangled web of multiple sales representatives and the complex billing and invoicing of spot purchases. However, the flexibility to tailor the message with a station announcer, local reference, or specific market promotion is diminished with the wired network buy.

Unwired Networks

To fill the need for convenient and creative national or multi-market buys, and at the same time provide the ease of network buying, "unwired" network divisions within The Interep Radio Store and the Katz Radio Group have evolved. For the agency media buyer, the unwired network buys provide spot flexibility with network's ease-of-buying and the opportunity to tailor specific market promotions because The Interep Radio Store or Katz Radio Group packages together all the stations an advertiser needs to effectively reach the target audience. The agency deals with one salesperson and receives one invoice, but the ads are placed with individual stations by The Interep Radio Store or the Katz Radio Group unwired network representative. The unwired network advertisements are not broadcast from one location to all affiliates, but rather, the advertiser or agency contracts with stations to run the ads during particular times or programs just as the station would run local spot ads.

The latest innovation in unwired networks is called "Radio Format Networks," a program introduced by The Interep Radio Store in 1991. The radio format networks are becoming very popular with advertisers because they pinpoint an advertiser's target with complete accuracy by grouping together similarly formatted stations like Country, Urban, or News/Talk all onto one radio network. In essence, radio format networks match life-style and consumption data to a specific format so the advertiser is assured of reaching the primary target.

Radio Advertising Is Big Business

According to the Radio Advertising Bureau, the revenues from radio advertising in the United States in 1993, were estimated at $9.6 billion: network radio accounting for $407 million; national spot coming in at $1.6 billion; and local/retail spots accounting for the largest portion—$7.5 billion. Though larger than the GNP of many small countries, radio still commands a very small share of the advertising dollar, particularly in the United States. In 1950 U.S. advertisers spent $332 million on spot and national advertising representing 10.6% of all the money spent on national advertising from all media (see Table 1–1). In the introductory years of television, radio's national revenues slumped and did not attain the same spending volume for fifteen years! During the same period radio's share of all national advertising dropped from 10.2% to 3.6%. National radio advertising once garnered 5.8% of all advertising dollars and today it is only 1.6% of the total: and although the late '80s and '90s have seen some large advertisers starting to, once again, heavily invest in radio advertising, there is still room for many other, large advertisers to utilize national radio.

Ironically, during the first thirty years of radio, national advertising dominated radio ad revenues, and it was not until the early 1950s that local ad revenues overtook national spending. Today local ad revenues greatly outpace national spending and account for over 75% of all radio expenditures.

Of course, to attain nearly $2 billion in radio spending means that there are many national advertisers in the United States using radio (see Table 1–2). For many advertisers on the list this expenditure represents a significant portion of their advertising dollars. For instance, in the United States for companies like Sears Roebuck & Co., Warner-Lambert & Co., K Mart Corp., and AT&T national radio advertising represents between 14.3% and 6.9% of their advertising budgets (see Table 1–2). Others, such as Ford Motor Co., Coca-Cola Co., Pepsico, and Procter and Gamble, are spending a far smaller fraction (less than 1.9%) of their advertising budgets on radio. For others not on the list at all, it is possible that neither agency nor client has given radio the attention it merits.

A Look Ahead

Radio is an extremely valuable advertising medium that provides the targeting capability and reach opportunities that large and small advertisers require. Options provided by the unwired networks further the flexibility to deliver broad, but still well-defined, audiences for advertisers.

Table 1–2

1993 Radio Advertising Expenditures of Selected Companies

	Network Radio (000)	National Spot Radio (000)	Radio's Percent of Total Advertising
U.S. Companies			
Sears Roebuck & Co.	$69,188.1	$15,940.9	14.3%
Warner-Lambert Co.	25,550.7	254.8	10.5
K Mart Corp.	11,553.0	18,753.4	10.3
Wrigley Wm Jr. Co	10,970.8	3054.9	11.8
AT&T	22,797.6	10,194.2	6.9
Campbell Soup Co.	2,401.3	677.5	3.2
Anheuser-Busch Co. Inc.	—	7,610.4	2.4
General Motors Corp.	15,434.4	9,422.3	2.3
Pepsico Inc.	—	11,855.1	1.9
Philip Morris Co. Inc.	5,610.3	12,095.2	1.8
Procter & Gamble	16,907.2	2,640.6	1.5
Coca-Cola Co.	1,413.0	1,155.5	1.4
Chrysler Corp.	4,723.0	929.7	0.96
Time Warner Inc.	1,394.7	1,432.8	0.7
Ford Motor Co.	2,670.8	1,354.5	0.6

Source: U.S.: Radio Advertising Bureau, provided by Competitive Media Reporting, 1994.

This book shows how to influence more customers by including radio in a media mix and offers in-depth case examples of some of the most successful radio ads in recent broadcast history. Using the strategy of media planning and the values of radio, the book focuses on the tactical message decisions that need to be made for radio commercials.

Chapter 2 looks specifically at radio in the context of media strategy starting with a brand, Betty Crocker, that experienced a conscious decision to shift media dollars into radio. The quantitative role and qualitative value of radio are presented in relation to other media. Finally, vignettes of advertisers who have used radio are presented in the context of their contribution to their overall media strategies.

Chapter 3 looks at the process of campaign planning using

Table 1–3

Top 20 National Radio Categories—1993, Ranked by Total

1993 Ranking	Spot Radio	Network Radio	Combined*
Retail	25.2%	20.4%	23.6%
Services (financial/ communications)	15.2	12.1	14.1
Automotive	8.9	6.5	8.1
Food (including restaurants)	6.4	9.0	7.5
Entertainment and Amusement	8.4	2.4	6.4
Drug Products	1.8	12.2	5.3
Travel	6.0	3.8	5.2
Confections/Snacks/Soft Drinks	3.6	7.7	5.0
Publishing and Media	3.9	4.8	4.2
Insurance and Real Estate	2.8	3.1	2.9
Beer and Wine	3.6	1.1	2.8
Gas and Oil	3.4	0.3	2.3
Computers and Office Equipment	2.2	1.5	2.0
Direct Response	0.6	4.7	2.0
Agriculture and Gardening	1.9	0.6	1.5
Consumer Electronics	0.4	2.2	1.2
Cosmetics and Toiletries	1.1	1.2	1.1
Home Furnishings	0.6	2.0	1.1
Apparel	1.2	0.4	0.9
Soaps and Cleaners	0.2	1.2	0.6
All Others	2.6	2.8	2.2
	100.0%	100.0%	100.0%

*Weighted average of raw dollar figures of spot and network radio.
Source: Radio Advertising Bureau from Competitive Media/LNA, full-year 1993.

three well-known ad campaigns: from the United States and Canada. In each case radio played an important, though not always dominant, role in the media mix. The cases illustrate the flexibility and power of radio and, most important, they help showcase the elements of the campaign planning process.

Chapter 4 shifts from the campaign and media decision to the tactical creative decisions and looks briefly at what is known about tactics that work in developing advertising messages. After seeing that most advertising prescriptions do not take product differences into consideration, the book takes a unique descriptive look at the most common styles and structures of radio commercials, broken down into major product groupings.

Chapters 5 through 8 look at what message features are found most commonly in good versus bad performing radio ads. The analysis—derived from the unique analysis of the data files from one of the largest radio pretesting companies—is conducted separately for the different product groupings and is the first such insight available for those developing radio ads. Over 2,000 ads from more than seventy product categories are used in the analysis. Case examples are highlighted throughout to aid in making the illustrations.

Finally, Chapter 9 summarizes radio's strengths and uses as discussed in the previous chapters, and gives a final, compelling look into the future of radio advertising. Several technological advances are brought to light to demonstrate how radio is well prepared to remain a major player in the advertising industry.

Chapter 2

Radio: A Uniquely Powerful Medium

Asked if she really had nothing on in the [calendar] photograph, Marilyn, her blue eyes wide, purred: "I had the radio on."
—Time, *August 11, 1952*

R adio's unique strengths are found in five important market-ing areas: reach, targetability, cost-efficiency, frequency, and creativity. When used correctly—with the proper station formats, radio copy, and correct dayparts—radio advertising has the unique ability to reach any number of highly selective demographic groups who, subsequently, may take actions (i.e., buy a product advertised on radio) to help increase an adver-tiser's buying line. Here's a breakdown of how radio's unique strengths can work for advertisers:

Reach

Radio is an omnipresent medium, people use it everywhere. Some advertising experts refer to it as the "ubiquitous medium"— the medium that is with consumers from the time they awaken in the morning until they go to bed at night. Today, there are over half a billion radios in use in the United States, or an average of six radios in over 99% of American households. The average weekly reach of persons older than twelve years is 96%, and this same group listens to radio for more than three hours each day.

It is easy to reach an advertiser's customer through radio because the typical American radio listener listens to only three radio stations each week: his or her preferred music station; a backup station for news and information; and third, a station determined by the listener's mood at the moment.[1] With such a small variance in audience listening patterns, advertisers can develop precise aim for their messages. Hence, once target markets are identified it is relatively simple to select the appropriate advertising vehicle with which to reach them. The acceptance of radio as part of our everyday life-style makes it an unobtrusive and effective advertising medium with the potential to reach market segments in a variety of buying situations. In fact, statistics show that except for prime time television, people turn to radio for entertainment and information more than any other medium (Figure 2–1).[2]

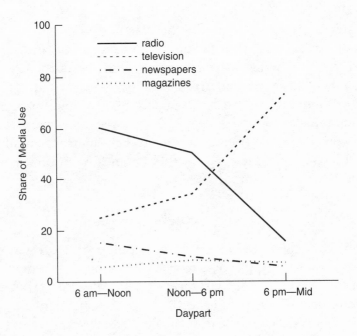

Figure 2–1

Share of Weekday Media Use Adults 25–54

From Schulberg (1992) using Media Targeting for the '90s.

Radio also scores high with the all-important measure of effective reach (when listeners are exposed to a message at least three times). In any given week radio has an effective reach of over 74%.[3] Additionally, radio has better reach for most dayparts than other media. Dayparts, or daily time segments, are broken down into Morning Drive (5:30 or 6:00 A.M. to 10:00 A.M.), Daytime (10:00 A.M. to 3:00 P.M.), Afternoon Drive (3:00 P.M. to 7:00 or 8:00 P.M.), Nighttime (7:00 or 8:00 P.M. to Midnight), and Overnight (Midnight until Morning Drive). Figure 2–2 shows radio's largest audience is during the morning and afternoon drives—the biggest audience during these timeframes compared to any other media. No other medium can claim the impressive reach numbers that are available with radio.

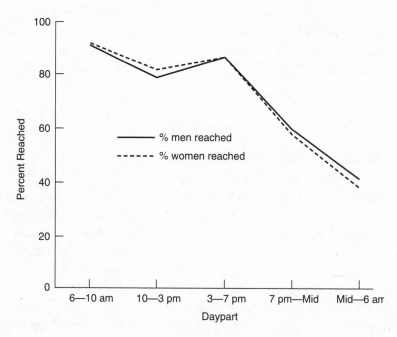

Figure 2–2

*Percent Reached by Daypart Men
and Women Older than 18*

From *Radio Fact Book*, 1993, and Schulberg 1992)

Timing Is Everything

Furthermore, those who listen to radio view it as the most useful advertising medium for information when they shop,[1] and there is strong evidence that consumer shopping and radio advertising exposure are much more proximate than for any other advertising medium. In other words, timing is everything and radio's prime listening hours coincide with U.S. consumers' peak shopping hours. Over 75% of all purchases take place between 6:00 A.M. and 7:00 P.M.—the hours when radio listening is at its highest. In addition, 55% of all consumers listen to radio within one hour of their largest purchase of the day.[4]

Drive-Time Listening

Radio is the ultimate commuting companion. Over 95% of the cars on the highway have a radio, and 97% percent of commuters listen to the radio during their drive.[1] But radio listening doesn't stop once a listener reaches his or her place of work because over 60% of working adults in the United States have a radio in their office.[1]

Targetability

Radio also has the unique ability to target and reach very specific audiences. Radio can be aimed at groups of people based on their demographics, where they live, their particular interests, or even by their psychological make-up. Target selection is achieved by placing advertisements on different radio formats at various times of the day, or by concentrating on different parts of the country. For example, an advertiser can reach 78.3% of adults aged eighteen to thirty-four with strategic placements on Classic Rock stations. And almost 58% of adults over fifty-five can be reached with Oldies or Lite Rock stations.[1] Sports enthusiasts can be reached with All Sports programming, news hounds with All News stations, or those who are politically inclined with Talk radio. The flexibility of target aim is limited only by the advertiser's foresight.

Radio's targetability and selectivity minimize message waste and allow marketers to tailor the creative aspects of their message to meet audience needs, desires, and life-styles. While other media have a certain degree of market selectivity, radio, by far, allows advertisers the most flexibility in audience selection (Table 2–1), which translates to increased cost-efficiency and more effective message strategies.

Western Union: A Targeting Success

Western Union, the company that pioneered the money transfer business over a century ago, utilizes radio's unique ability to specifically target a primary audience with pinpoint accuracy. In the late 1980s, Western Union wanted to expand its International Service to make instant money transfers available around the world. After careful evaluation of its potential customer base, the company discovered that ethnic workers seeking to wire money to family in their native countries were the most frequent users of its International Money Transfer service. In the fall of 1991, Western Union selected radio as the main component of its advertising campaign because of the medium's ability to effectively target and deliver specific audiences. In Chicago, Polish language radio was chosen; New York consisted of buys on Caribbean, Polish, and Hispanic stations; and Caribbean radio was bought in Toronto and Montreal to reach Jamaicans, Haitians, and Guyanese sending money to the Caribbean.

"Since there are only a limited number of programs on selected Polish, Hispanic, and Caribbean radio stations, the listenership is highly concentrated during the time the Western Union ads air," according to the Vice President/Account Supervisor at Lowe & Partners/SMS Western Union's agency-of-record. And, Western Union's Director of International Marketing said, "The only way we can effectively reach many of our key international customers is through radio that's programmed to their specific needs."

Through the use of highly targeted radio, Western Union

Table 2–1

Media Selectivity

Media	Geographic	Demographic	Special Interest	Psychological
Outdoor				
Highway	* * * * *	* * *		
Street	* * * * *	* * * *		
Station	* * * * *	* * *	*	
In-car	* * * * *	* *		
Point of Sale	* * * * *		* * *	
Newspaper	* * * * *	* *	*	
Television				
Spot				
Daytime	* * * *	* * *	*	*
Fringe	* * * *	* * *	* *	* *
Prime	* * * *	* * *	*	*
Network				
Daytime	* *	* *	*	*
Fringe	* *	* *	* *	* *
Prime	* *	* *	*	*
Cable	* * * *	* *	* * * *	* * * * *
Radio				
Spot	* * * * *	* * * *	* * * * *	* * * *
Network	* * * * *	* * *	* * *	* * *
Magazines				
General	*	* * * *	* * * *	* * *
Trade	*	* * *	* * * * *	* *
Special Interest		* *	* * * * *	* * * *
Direct Mail	* * * * *	* * * * *	* * * * *	* * * * *

*Denotes level of selectivity.
Source: Baker, Stephen, (1979), *Systematic Approach to Advertising Creativity,* New York: McGraw-Hill. Adapted from Doyle Dane Bernbach, Chicago and New York.

International's transactions have grown 100%, totally exceeding all expectations. "Radio will continue to be a key player in Western Union International's ad campaign," said Lowe & Partners/SMS Vice President/Account Supervisor.[4]

Political Targeting with Radio

Even politicians have discovered that radio is the most effective way to sell ideas to constituencies. For example, the 1990 gubernatorial race in Connecticut brought many changes to the state: an independent, Lowell Weicker, was elected for the first time since 1854, and an innovative, statewide radio advertising campaign played a key role in helping Weicker become governor. With marketing strategy assistance from Gold & Ward, an Avon, Connecticut-based firm, Weicker was the first candidate ever to have localized, almost personalized, radio spots airing in various markets throughout the state.

"For the best possible reach and targeting, we divided the state into its major markets—Hartford/New Haven, and Fairfield County—and a number of small markets including New London, Torrington, Danbury, and Greenwich," explained Peter Gold, President of Gold & Ward. "We then pulled precise economic facts and figures for the small markets and scripted four different radio spots tailored for each region."

From October 1, 1990 until Election Day, radio listeners in each smaller market heard unique, sixty-second spots with economic information pertinent only to their own hometowns. The spots opened with an overview of the market's current economic situation and concluded with candidate Weicker discussing how he hoped to address the economic issues—*specific* for each market. The spots ran on several News/Talk and Adult Contemporary AM stations in the small markets, and on several FM stations with greater reach in the larger markets.

"While television seems to be the most widely-used method of political advertising and is important, I believe radio provides an advantage because of its intrinsic targeting capabilities," said Gold "Governor Weicker's campaign has proven that radio reaches people—in *every* market—with the information that is strictly important to them!"[5]

Cost-Efficiency

Radio can often be the most cost-efficient medium for an advertiser or agency to purchase. When compared on a cost per thousand (cpm) basis, radio has consistently ranked as one of the most efficient media. Whereas the cost of newspapers has climbed to almost $20 cpm, radio, on the average, has remained at less than $3 cpm and over the last decade, radio has had the smallest price increase of any major medium (Figure 2–3). In fact, along with outdoor advertising, network and spot radio advertising are the only advertising venues whose price increases were less than the Consumer Price Index (CPI).[1]

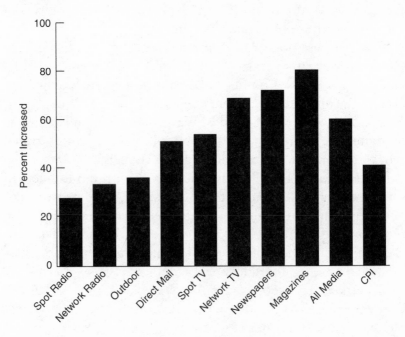

Figure 2–3

*Cost per Thousand Increase of Major Media
1982–1993*

From *Radio Facts*, 1993

Radio spots are also relatively inexpensive to produce. While it is not unusual to see production costs for a thirty-second television commercial exceed $100,000, a similar length radio commercial rarely costs more than a few thousand dollars. The lower costs of production associated with radio do not affect its ability to communicate selling messages because recent studies show that there is virtually no difference in audience recall between the best radio advertisements and the best television advertisements.[6]

Frequency

Radio has also been called the "frequency medium" because it can achieve extremely high frequencies in very short periods of time.[7] For example, given the same budget radio can hit a market segment at least twenty times more often than television. Using RADAR data in an advertisement touting their radio network, CBS compared the frequencies of radio to television. The advertisement, from the early 1980s, hypothetically compares two $30 million media budgets: one television and one radio campaign. The ad shows that a budget of this size will buy three or four network commercials per week on a top-rated television program—or about 150 to 200 commercials a year. On the other hand, with the same budget, the radio campaign buys 200 network commercials a *week,* with an overlay of twenty announcements per week on four radio stations in each of the 100 key markets.

Creativity

Radio lets advertisers generate an unlimited number of mental images. Some media experts suggest that the "magic" of radio lets listeners use their imagination as it stimulates a "theater of the mind." The mental images that are created by a radio audience are not encumbered or restricted by the visual limitations of television. Radio has the ability to stimulate "great visual enhancement" and allow listeners to use their imagination to form their own mental images. Simply put, imagery is the process that people use to develop "pictures in the mind."[8] Stimuli received through the five senses enable listeners to evoke thought processes that lead to images shaped from their own experiences.[9] Therefore, the thoughts and ideas generated are consistent with the listeners' personal views of life and the way they perceive their environment. There is strong evidence that thought-provoking imagery can lead to higher message recall and learning of product-related information because radio listeners remember the advertiser's product in a way that is strictly personal to them.[10]

There are a number of ways in which a talented copywriter can stimulate mental imagery among audience members. The most common methods include advertisements that use "concrete image-provoking words" that simply direct the audience to think of an image. To illustrate, consider the images that evolve when a commercial describes a "beautiful summer day with white clouds floating in a blue sky," or when a commercial asks listeners to "imagine that you are relaxing on a beach watching the ten-foot waves roll onto the shore." For each of these messages, radio listeners can easily conjure up a scene to fit their own experience. Messages that place the advertised product into the imagined scene will have higher recall and stronger learning effects. Radio commercials that stimulate audience imagery may be more memorable and effective than other media that use visual formats: while the mental pictures developed from magazine and television visual messages are restricted to the parameters of the advertisements, the images generated from radio imagery are virtually unlimited.

Not only does radio prompt listeners to create their own images, it enables people to transfer the images seen in television commercials.[11] A recent study has shown that audiences can easily picture the visual images seen in a television commercial to corresponding radio commercials. This "imagery transfer" means that advertisers can increase budget and campaign effectiveness with an appropriate blend of television and radio commercials.

Other studies have found that the imagery stimulated by radio can also "strengthen the emotional response to a commercial, create a more favorable attitude toward the commercial and enhance behavioral intentions."[10,12] These studies show radio to be a strong marketing tool and an invaluable element of the media mix. It leads to more effective and efficient advertising campaigns and emphasizes the importance of an integrated and comprehensive media plan.

Selling the Sporty Life-Style with Creative Imagery

In the late 1980s, Chevrolet used radio as its only advertising medium to rejuvenate the image of the Camaro. When Chevrolet introduced the Camaro to America in the mid-1970s, Southern California—with its "sporty" life-style and miles of golden beaches—was chosen as the initial roll-out market. The Camaro sold very well for about ten or twelve years but, eventually, the novelty and magic of the car wore off. Chevrolet needed to freshen its ad campaign and turned to radio with the assistance of Chuck Blore, CEO of The Chuck Blore Company, a Hollywood, California-based radio production company.

"Chevrolet came to us to help re-marry the image of the Camaro with the Southern California life-style and felt that radio—particularly in an area where so many depend on their cars and listen to the radio while stuck in traffic—was the perfect place to promote their product," Blore explained. With that in mind, Blore wrote and created a series of sixty-second spots, running from 1988 until 1991, with the tagline of "Life seems a little bit better in a Camaro by Chevrolet." The creative spots, geared to adults aged eighteen to thirty-five, placed listeners in the driver's seat of their own Camaro and spoke of carefree days and nights that just might be possible by owning a Camaro. Blore based the campaign on the idea that many people, at one time in their lives, have pictured themselves driving off in a sporty car to escape their everyday troubles. Radio, unencumbered with pictures dictated by the creative director of a television campaign, allowed radio listeners to picture themselves—

with their own unique look and personality—driving around in a Chevy Camaro.

"During the first six months of the campaign, which initially ran only in Southern California, Camaro sales jumped 60%. The campaign then expanded to include approximately eleven states on the West Coast and sales continued to increase," said Blore.[13] [COMMERCIAL 1 ON DISC]

Radio Imagery Reaches Out and Touches

In the late 1970s, AT&T was searching for an effective way to increase long-distance telephone usage because market research had revealed that many of their customers saw long-distance calls as little more than a price bulge at the bottom of their phone bill each month. Seeking the creative assistance of Chuck Blore, the first national radio ad campaign—entitled "Feelings"—promoted the idea that long-distance calling was the best way to get close to someone special who lived far away.

Blore's initial radio spot for the campaign brought home the idea that it's OK to pick up the phone when you miss the sound of someone's voice—and, the spots said, it was really not that expensive to make the call. The following year, Don Wood wrote the now famous "Reach Out and Touch Someone" lyrics that became the AT&T "theme" for over ten years. According to Blore, "AT&T conducted another survey just five years into the radio campaign and found a 98% turnaround—in other words, long-distance telephone usage increased as consumers were listening to their 'feelings' to 'Reach Out and Touch Someone' special who may have lived across the country or around the world."[13] [COMMERCIAL 2 ON DISC]

Radio in the Media Mix

Radio is an important element of the media mix, allowing advertisers to achieve their desired reach and frequency, and to create motivating, easily recalled images at cost-effective prices. But radio has the advantage of complementing other advertising media as well. Advertisers should not rely on just one medium to advertise their products but should strive to achieve media "synergy," because radio hits audience segments that other media miss. For example, very light television viewers (those who watch less than forty minutes a day) listen to the radio for more than three-and-a-half hours a day. Radio also reaches those people that newspapers miss. On the average, radio reaches over 88% of non-readers of newspaper.[1]

Media Imperatives

To determine the reach of individual and combinations of media, advertisers have adopted the use of a series of media statistics known as media imperatives. Media imperatives contrast and compare the audience coverage between two types of media and categorize media use into four distinct categories:

Dual imperative	Heavy use of both media
Media #1 imperative	Heavy use of media #1—light use of media #2
Media #2 imperative	Heavy use of media #2—light use of media #1
Non-imperative	Light use of both media

The categories can be matched with market demographics or product use. Audience profiles can be identified and the appropriate media plan and budget developed. To illustrate, suppose 52% of the male users of a particular deodorant were radio imperative. If an advertiser were to use a television-only plan, over half of the target would not be reached. Advertisers can determine budget distribution accordingly and actually get more "bang for their advertising dollar."

Imperatives allow radio's targetability to be put to efficient use and acquire more complete market coverage and reach of segments of the audience who might not otherwise receive the message. The information given by the media imperatives underscores the necessity of a multi-media approach and reinforces the importance of radio as part of the total media plan.

Strategic Examples

The following two cases illustrate how radio can be used in the media mix. The media plan in the first case uses radio as a complement to the prime message carrier: television. In this case radio acts as supplementary medium to increase reach and frequency numbers. The second case illustrates how radio advertising can function as the principal message carrier in an advertising campaign.

CASE 1: MEDIA PLAN FOR BETTY CROCKER FROSTING

The Product: Betty Crocker Frosting—a ready-to-use cake frosting that comes in a variety of flavors and is used at home.

Target Market: The defined primary target market includes women aged twenty-five to forty-nine who live in households with five or more people. According to the Simmons Marketing Research Bureau, this segment represents over 70% of the users.

Media Objectives: The company decided to have a year-round national campaign with a special emphasis on the fall/winter holiday "Baking Season." The plan called for a broad exposure that would reflect the reach and frequency levels of the competing brands.

Media Strategy and Tactics: The media strategy was designed to hit the target audience with a 90+ reach and a 3+ frequency. The overall media plan included:

- Primary medium
- Secondary medium
- Continuity
- Supplementary media
- Day/prime network TV
- Network radio/syndicated radio
- 52-week continuity
- Tactical magazines

The media plan called for flights of two weeks on and two off, for a total of eleven flights. The budget was divided into two timeframes, with 55% of the budget spent in the first half of the fiscal year and 45% spent in the second half. The dollars allocated per medium were as follows:

TV	76%
Radio	19%
Print	5%

Media Imperatives: The media imperatives show that if the campaign were to use television only, almost 31% of the market would not be reached (Figure 2–4). The imperatives indicate that newspapers cannot reach 30.7% of the market and magazines cannot reach 27.8% of the market.[14]

CASE 2: MEDIA PLAN FOR MOLSON GOLDEN ALE (see related success story on page 136)

The Product: An imported upscale ale consumed in homes and in bars and restaurants.

Target Market: Molson defined their primary target market as men of legal drinking age to thirty-four years old, who are college educated, and who earn more than $20,000 per year. Research from the Simmons Market Research shows that over 50% of the Molson users have attended or graduated college and over 73% of them earn at least $30,000.

Research data shows the share of time that this market spends each day on each major medium to be:

Radio	49%
Television	38%
Newspapers	8%
Magazines	5%

Radio—Television Contrast

Dual Imperative 20.6%	Radio Imperative 30.6%
Television Imperative 35.5%	Non-Imperative 13.3%

Radio—Newspaper Contrast

Dual Imperative 23.2%	Radio Imperative 30.7%
Newspaper Imperative 31.5%	Non-Imperative 14.6%

Radio—Magazine Contrast

Dual Imperative 25.4%	Radio Imperative 27.8%
Magazine Imperative 34.1%	Non-Imperative 12.7%

Radio—Outdoor Contrast

Dual Imperative 21.4%	Radio Imperative 33.4%
Outdoor Imperative 30.4%	Non-Imperative 14.8%

Figure 2–4
Media Imperatives for Betty Crocker Frosting Users
From Simmons Marketing Research Bureau, 1990.

Media Objectives: The company's plan was to have a year-round national advertising campaign with special attention given to the peak summer months. The objective was to maintain brand awareness and "top of mind" numbers with adequate reach and frequency values.

Media Strategy and Tactics: The plan called for advertisements to run on 200 radio stations in ninety markets. The creative copy used "soft-sell" humor with a touch of "clever, sexually charged repartee" to convey the Molson name. Radio was the primary message carrier.

Media Imperatives: Research indicated that this target was a heavy user of radio. In fact, on the average, this target segment spent more time listening to radio than any other medium. The media imperatives indicate that if television were the sole message carrier, 30.6% of the target would not be reached (Figure 2–5). Furthermore, if either magazines or

Radio—Television Contrast

Dual Imperative 19.4%	Radio Imperative 30.6%
Television Imperative 32.6%	Non-Imperative 17.4%

Radio—Newspaper Contrast

Dual Imperative 22.9%	Radio Imperative 23.8%
Newspaper Imperative 42.2%	Non-Imperative 11.1%

Radio—Magazine Contrast

Dual Imperative 27.7%	Radio Imperative 23.4%
Magazine Imperative 34.5%	Non-Imperative 14.4%

Radio—Outdoor Contrast

Dual Imperative 23.7%	Radio Imperative 23.8%
Outdoor Imperative 39.1%	Non-Imperative 13.4%

Figure 2–5

Media Imperatives for Molson Golden Ale Users

From Simmons Marketing Research Bureau, 1990.

newspapers were used as the sole message carrier, 23.4% and 23.8% of the market would not be reached.[15,16]

A Frequent Misconception About Radio

As with all media, radio does have a perceived "flaw." One criticism sometimes directed toward radio is its fragmented reach. However, fragmentation is radio's greatest strength because fragmentation *is* targetability. There's little waste with radio. With radio, an advertiser can target by age, sex, income, occupation, ethnic background, geographics, life-style. Or, the advertiser can target anyone under 18, women 25 to 49, men 28 to 34, or adults over 55 very easily just by choosing the proper format to advertise a product.

The proliferation of radio has contributed to its fragmentation. Aside from the fact that, as previously stated, there are almost 10,000 radio stations in the United States, it is not unusual to find five times as many radio stations as television stations in a given market and a number of different programming formats.[1] The ratings for any given type of format range from 1.5 for Lite Rock to 17.7 for Contemporary Hit Radio (CHR) stations. When the proper formats are chosen for a particular buy, an advertiser can reach the target based on audience composition and ratings.

Not Enough Sex Appeal?

So if radio advertising is so good and offers so many formats and avenues with which to reach listeners, why don't more advertisers use it? Why is it that consumers spend more then one-third of their media time listening to the radio, yet radio receives only 7% of the advertising dollars?[1] Information Resources Inc., a leading market research firm, was commissioned by The Interep Radio Store a few years ago to conduct a study of the advertising agency attitudes of nearly 400 executives representing approximately fifty agencies across the country. The studies list some of the perceptions that advertising executives have to-

Table 2-2
Reach by Station Format

Station Format	Percent of Stations	Average Rating	5-Day Reach (%)	Effective Reach (%)
Country	26.8	14.4	31.11	11.89
Adult Contemporary	16.6	13.4	19.75	4.37
CHR/Rock	5.5	11.3	28.20	8.09
News/Talk/Business	7.1	7.4	17.64	5.51
Album Oriented	4.1	7.1	19.75	4.37
Golden Oldies	7.5	4.6	13.27	2.70
Easy Listening	1.6	3.5	10.24	1.92
Religious	8.7	3.1	8.82	1.81
Middle of the Road	4.3	2.5	6.77	1.64
Urban/Black	3.2	2.9	8.82	1.51
Classical	.5	2.6	7.81	1.33
Classic Rock	2.1	2.3	6.85	1.29
Lite/Soft Contemp	3.3	2.3	7.12	1.06
Spanish	3.5	NA	NA	NA
Jazz	.5	NA	NA	NA
Variety/Others	5.1	NA	NA	NA

NA = Data not available.
Source: Compiled from *Radio Facts Book* (1993) and Simmons Marketing Research Bureau (1990)

ward radio and go far in explaining why radio is not used more often. Some of the reasons given for not using radio include:

• Radio is not as "sexy" as other media.
• It is difficult to buy because of the number of stations involved.
• Radio is not as exciting as other media.
• Radio is a local medium only.
• Agency creative teams prefer to work in television.
• It is difficult to convince clients of radio's value.
• Radio is not suited for all products.

Others suggest that radio's lack of use can be traced to the advertising agencies themselves. It has been suggested that some agencies avoid radio because "it isn't lucrative (and) isn't as visible in the industry." Other agencies don't appreciate the impact and importance of radio and often distribute radio creative assignments to inexperienced junior personnel.[17] This approach to radio advertising often leads to a lack of creativity or "copycat" commercials.[18] Some agencies have responded to this problem by designating a radio creative director in each creative group.[17] Others are using radio boutiques to help write, cast, and produce radio commercials. Many of these special radio shops, such as Joy Radio, The Chuck Blore Company, and Bert Berdis and Company, will be mentioned in various case studies throughout this book. The bottom line is that many agencies are beginning to recognize the value of radio and have taken active steps to ensure its place in the media mix.

Summary

To conclude on a positive note, Jack Myers, president of Parsippany, NJ–based Myers Marketing and Research, one of the nation's leading research firms which chronicles the changes that occur in media and advertising, conducts a yearly survey of over 600 advertiser and agency executives to assess their opinions on various media characteristics. In a recent study, entitled "Survey on Marketing Effectiveness and Media Accountability," the advertising community was asked to judge network and spot radio, broadcast and spot TV, cable network TV, newspapers, direct mail, FSI's, outdoor, and in-store advertising. Radio was judged very effective compared to all other media in the following categories:

- **Targets specific audiences.** Spot radio ranked very high in this category with direct mail, and cable network TV as the only media of the ten rated to score higher.
- **Price-efficiency.** As stated earlier in the chapter, during these days of ever-changing budgetary restrictions, radio comes out a winner. Outranked only by cable network TV, network and spot radio are the leaders in this category.

- **Provides value-added promotional support.** It is very difficult for any other media to outrank radio in this category.
In fact, radio's promotional ability is directly related to its
ability to interact with an audience. For example, if a
local radio personality is airing a morning program live
from a car dealership on a Saturday morning, loyal listeners of that personality respond by attending the event.
This rapid success was experienced by Tauder Ford, Inc.,
located outside of Philadelphia in Phoenixville, Pennsylva-
nia, when the Ford dealer decided to hold a last-minute
sale to clear out overloaded inventory. Over the seven-day
period of Tauder Ford's "mega sale" they ran twenty-
eight sixty-second informational spots on Philadelphia's
country radio station, WXTU FM, encouraging listeners
to stop by the dealership, particularly during a live-remote
during the last day of the sale. Fifteen vehicles sold as a result of the live radio remote and intense radio schedule,
and every Tauder salesperson was booked with customers
during the remote. According to the vice president of Tauder Ford, "The radio schedule and promotion we ran
were tremendous traffic builders. We will continue to use
radio in our future advertising plans."[19]

In conclusion, as evidenced by the information presented earlier in the chapter and later in this book, radio is an important
and efficient part of the media mix, which can either act as the
prime message carrier or supplement other media. Radio's
strengths fit well into the total media plan where advertising
campaigns should be defined as to what is best in achieving exposure, reach, frequency, creativity, and message recall, and
communicating the selling message.

Chapter 3

Putting Radio in Your Plan

Advertisements are now so numerous that they are negligently perused, and it has therefore become necessary to gain attention by magnificence of promises, and by eloquences sometimes sublime and sometimes pathetic.

—Samuel Johnson, 1759

The unequivocal conclusion from chapters 1 and 2 is that radio is being underutilized by advertisers and that radio has important qualities that beg for it to be included in campaign planning. The decision of whether to use radio advertising begins with the broader advertising planning done for the brand when advertisers and agencies set goals, strategy, and tactics. The planning document becomes the blueprint that unifies the Customer, Product, and Competition. A successful advertising plan examines each of these factors and translates them into action. The advertising planning document helps assure that the positioning, media, and creative choices are in sync with one another and with company resources and strategy. For radio advertising this planning document both imposes the limits and defines the needs that radio advertising may or may not be able to serve.

The following is a typical blueprint for campaign planning and provides the format to look at three successful radio case studies.

I. SITUATION ANALYSIS

A. Product Analysis. What are the tangible and intangible benefits of the product or brand that make it unique and salient from the customer's viewpoint?

In many cases product benefits can be communicated effectively by using the imagery of radio discussed in the previous chapter. Even intangible benefits like friendship and caring effectively conveyed in AT&T's "Reach Out and Touch Someone" campaign are possible in radio. Radio ads for well-known products like McDonald's, Coca-Cola, and Pepsi generally reinforce benefits that customers are already aware of. When the American Egg Board wanted to emphasize tangible benefits of price and value, they shifted their media mix by increasing radio from 7% to 31% of the total media budget.

B. Customer Analysis. Who are the current or potential consumers? Why do they or might they buy? Is the purchase risky or important to consumers? Are the product features of the product salient to any group of consumers?

A powerful feature of radio is the ability to target consumers. The Western Union example in the previous chapter highlighted ethnic targeting through radio and the Weicker campaign for governor illustrates geographic targeting can work. The range of radio formats and programs aimed at different life-styles and age groups offers another adaptation. Yet another opportunity to target is the segmentation by daypart that offers an advertiser access to the business commuter, teen, or homemaker. Specific programming even provides even more focused access to sports fanatics, people concerned with their finances, car buffs, or a myriad of other audiences delivered by the array of programs aired in the United States and Canada.

The perceptions of risk in purchasing products vary considerably from low risk with a can of soup or candy bar to high risk in buying a washing machine or new fashion clothes. In addition, the motivation for purchasing can vary from very utilitarian such as that can of soup and the washer to more hedonistic or experiential in the case of the fashion clothing and candy bar.

C. Competitive and Market Analysis. Who will we take business from? Who is our direct and indirect competition from the customer's viewpoint? What is the marketing presence of our competition? How do we compare on salient benefits with the competition? What (if any) are the economic, market, environmental, and political-legal trends that could affect the product? Will the campaign be local, regional, national, or international?

Knowing what competitors are doing is helpful but does not always tell you to compete head on in the same media as your rivals. Blue Nun wine, which is discussed later in this chapter, chose not to compete head on with its competitors by advertising on television. Instead they shifted the focus to radio where they stood alone.

On a geographic basis radio offers tremendous flexibility. In addition to local stations and the traditional wired networks, the newer unwired networks mentioned in chapter 1 offer the ability to roll out in a highly efficient way that does not outrun your distribution or budget.

D. Company Resources and Goals. What is the company able to invest in money and effort in advertising the product? Is the product aimed at growth or at maintaining market share?

As the last chapter pointed out, radio is affordable and cost-effective from both a production and a media buying perspective. Products with small advertising budgets like Blue Nun can develop an effective national spot campaign without breaking the bank. For products that need to broaden their markets, the media imperative analysis in the last chapter illustrates that neglecting radio in the media mix eliminates a significant proportion of the audience from exposure to the campaign.

II. ADVERTISING STRATEGY

A. Advertising Objectives and Goals. Is the goal to capture awareness, remind, tease, create interest, inform, create image, persuade, or move to immediate action?

Radio advertising is, of course, adaptable to accomplish any of these objectives whether for the goal of capturing Chevrolet Camaros connection with the image of Southern California or persuading voters that Lowell Weicker had something relevant to offer their community.

B. Positioning. A statement of the "mental clarity" that the product should achieve in the customer's mind relative to competitive offerings. Ultra-Brite toothpaste has established a mental clarity in the consumer's mind relative to other products as the toothpaste that whitens your teeth. Consider the niche brand Pearl Drops aimed specifically to provide a clarity relative to toothpaste competition for those who smoke.

Positioning is the centerpiece of the advertising strategy and always is set before the tactics are developed and scripts written.

C. General Budgeting Outline. The total advertising allocation for the year is established. Here or in the media section of the plan the allocation is then subdivided by media (radio, newspaper, magazine, TV, etc.) and timing of the spending during the year.

III. CREATIVE STRATEGY AND TACTICS

A. Copy Platform. Translates the positioning strategy into a series of creative statements that become the campaign theme. The theme is a catchphrase that embodies the clarity of the desired positioning.

The theme for Ultra-Brite is the "Sex Appeal Toothpaste" while Pearl Drops is the "Smoker's Toothpolish." Both themes help establish their respective positions.

Chevrolet's "Heartbeat of America" campaign is the theme that executes the position of cars fit for nostalgic all-American life-styles.

AT&T's "Reach Out and Touch Someone" is the theme that solidifies the sentimental position of the long-distance call as the way to renew friendships and family relationships.

B. Develop Ad Executions. Once the positioning and creative platform is set, the job of developing the message style and structure begins. Many different executions can and often are explored to develop the right execution. Should we use 30″ or 60″ ads? What should be the format? The style? Will music help? The second half of this book focuses on the message structure, style, and presenter variables that go into the execution.

IV. MEDIA STRATEGY AND TACTICS

A. Media Objectives and Goals. What are the reach and frequency targets? What are the qualitative features of media needed? Can the audience be reached effectively and efficiently with all media?

The reach and frequency goals are the tangible quantitative targets: for example, 50% net reach over a four-week period with an average frequency of 4.5.

Radio today more than at any time can be tailored to the objective of narrow targeting with high average frequency or the moderate reach to mass audiences with intense or light frequency. As the centerpiece of a product's campaign, radio can achieve these goals, but more generally, radio as a supporting media can both broaden net reach and increase average frequency because of its favorable cost-efficiency.

The qualitative features are objectives for the product not easily represented in cold numbers. Does it need imagery? Is there synergy with other media? Is it affordable to create variations of the ad? Does the product need a longer format?

These, among many others, are examples of the qualitative strengths that radio provides.

The issues of target audience coverage and efficiency are crucial to the media planning. As pointed out in chapter 2, radio offers the ability to target but also the flexibility to combine stations in a media plan to provide broad coverage.

B. Inter- and Intra-Media Decisions. Which media categories (radio vs. newspaper) will be used and which media vehicles (night syndicated talk radio vs. daytime CBS radio news on the hour):

A McDonald's television campaign with theme music and slice-of-life scenario can easily achieve high reach and frequency given enough media dollars. Consider that the same dollars spent with perhaps 25% allocated to radio for ads run close to mealtimes would achieve greater reach, higher average frequency, and have greater overall impact because many people will actually be in their cars making decisions about where to have a meal. The result is a more effective campaign. This is the challenge presented to campaign planners—to break away from the media biases of the past and get more out of the dollars that are spent.

To illustrate the campaign planning process and demonstrate how three companies worked radio into their advertising plans in a creative and cost-effective manner, three examples are used: from the United States, Schieffelin & Co.'s Blue Nun and the American Egg Board, and from Canada, Nutri/System. In all three cases radio advertising was a critical part of the campaigns. Blue Nun had a media budget of just $1,500,000 but allocated over 99% primarily to spot with some network radio advertising. From 1977 until 1980, the American Egg Board allocated between 7% and over 30% of its more than $3 million ad budget to network radio. In 1993, the American Egg Board once again became a heavy radio advertiser with 16% of its $4.5 million budget invested in network radio. When Nutri/System in Canada began using radio in 1986, listener responses to their special offers and programs increased by as much as

300%. For each campaign, there is a breakdown of the planning process to both illustrate and highlight the different needs of the products.

Although the Blue Nun Wine campaign began in the 1970s, it is examined in length here because it is a classic case history of how a comprehensive, effective media plan, and its accompanying research on the competition and current playing field, will work hard to increase sales for an advertiser.

Blue Nun Wine

The Blue Nun ad campaign, which began in 1970 and continued for over a decade, achieved tremendous sales success for the brand as well as numerous awards for creativity and efficiency for its creators.[1]

I. SITUATION ANALYSIS

Blue Nun has been produced by Sichel of Germany for 200 years and has been imported in the United States since 1933 by Schieffelin and Co.—an importer of over a dozen wines and spirits. Case sales in 1978 reached 1,100,000 cases and had shown consistent 20% to 25% increases over the past years.

Product. Blue Nun is a premium Rhine wine, "pale golden in color with an excellent balance of sugar and acid, making it a round and extremely pleasing wine. It is a Liebfraumilch made from carefully selected Riesling, Sylvaner, and Muller-Thurgau grapes. It is a refreshing wine that combines elegance with body, fruitiness with charm, and is quite low in alcohol" (10% by volume). It is sold in cases of 12 with a 24-ounce size, 24 with a 12-ounce size, 6 with a 52-ounce size (Blue Nun and Sparkling Blue Nun), and 48 per case in a 6.5-ounce screw-top bottle (also sold in 3-pack).

Wine consumption in the United States began increasing in 1963, and 1977 it increased 5.1% to just over $3 billion. Table wine represented 69.1% of total wine sales of which 55% was red and rosé and the other 45% made up of the increasingly popular white wines. Imported table wines accounted for only 16.1% of U.S. consumption. During the late 1960s and early 1970s the 18 to 34 youth market led the growth toward wines, but the 18 to 34 market was beginning to shrink. The 25 to 44 market was growing rapidly.

Sociologists predicted a shift away from "hard" liquor toward wines. The 25 to 44 "youthful minded" group know more about wine than previous generations. Further research indicated people were becoming aware of the medical ramifications of using hard liquor and the low-calorie value of wine. Women were becoming more dominant in the purchase, deciding when to serve, where to buy, and what to choose. Selection was based upon price, the advice of friends, and having tasted the wine in the past.

Competition. Any beverage consumed with a meal could be considered competitive for table wines. The average American consumed twenty times more beer, coffee, and soft drinks and even five times as much tea. Directly competitive brands of table wine came from two firms, Almaden and Inglenook. Foreign rivals included Lancers, Mateus, and Bolla.

Market Trends	1970	1977
Total gallons	255.90	390.40
Import gallons	206.0	59.10
Per capita gallons	1.26	1.80
Consumption of cases (*millions*)	45.00	94.00
Consumer spending (*millions*)	$1,450	$3,000

White wine consumption was expected to increase 5% in 1978.

II. ADVERTISING STRATEGY

Marketing Objective. Continue increase in case sales of from 20% to 25%. Increase share of white wine consumption from 3.3% share in gallons.

Advertising Objective. Further establish brand awareness and product identity. Use focus groups to examine attitudes toward Blue Nun and its advertising.

Target Market. Men and women living in urban areas between the ages of 18 and 34. A secondary group was between 35 and 52. Many had attended college and were married. Geographically 37.8% of heavy users of imported table wines were in New York, Los Angeles, Chicago, San Francisco, and Texas. Heavy users entertain two to four people once or twice a month and dine out frequently.

Positioning. Blue Nun is an imported wine that people can be comfortable with and sure about, it is a name anyone can pronounce, and it goes well with any food.

Media Advertising Budget. 1977 budget was $1,511,290 and 1978 $2,000,000. Allocation at the industry average of $3 to $4 per case.

Rollout. In 1970 advertising was focused in New York. Los Angeles, and San Francisco followed in 1971 by New England, Oregon, and Washington State. Five markets per year were to be added, moving from the coasts inward.

Other Promotions. Letters to dealers announcing ad schedules and occasional public relations releases about Sichel of Germany, the annual "German Vintage Report," and a special story when Blue Nun passed the million case mark.

III. CREATIVE STRATEGY AND TACTICS

Creative Objective. All-purpose dinner wine that goes as well with meat as it does with fish.

Tactics. Used a humorous tone as a departure from competitors that used serious brand superiority, price, or education. Ann Meara and Jerry Stiller were selected as most effective from at least eight potential celebrity presenters.

Basic Claim. Delicious, imported, correct with any dish.

Format. Use humorous radio dialogue between entertaining characters.

Slogan. "Blue Nun is a delicious imported white wine that's correct with any dish."

Creative Example. A Clio-winning radio commercial that is one of twenty-six radio ads developed by 1978:

ANNOUNCER: Stiller and Meara

MEARA: Good evening, sir, I'm here for a poll.

STILLER: I don't think I have one. Could you use a ladder?

MEARA: No, I'm testing the political climate in your building.

STILLER: Come on in, doll, the air conditioner is on high.

MEARA: First question. Do you think most of Congress is on the take?

STILLER: Congress is on the Potomac. Everyone knows that.

MEARA: What do you think of the President's cabinet?

STILLER: A little too fancy for my tastes. I prefer Danish Modern.

MEARA: Mister, your political naiveté is incomprehensible.

STILLER: Thank you. I try to stay informed. Throw me another one. I'm hot now.

MEARA: Would you ever consider splitting your ticket?

STILLER: No, but I'd consider splitting my lamb chops. Why don't you join me for dinner, beautiful? We could even split some white wine.

MEARA: White wine with lamb chops?

STILLER: Sure, I've got a little Blue Nun in the kitchen.

MEARA: Oh, maybe she'll answer my questions on church and state.

STILLER: No, no. Blue Nun is a wine. A delicious imported wine that's correct with any dish. It goes as well with meat as it does with fish.

MEARA: Gee, what you lack in political savvy you more than make up for in culinary expertise.

STILLER: Culinary expertise? What's he running for?

ANNOUNCER: Blue Nun. The delicious white wine that's correct with any dish. Imported by Schieffelin & Co., New York.

IV. MEDIA STRATEGY AND TACTICS

Media Goal. Achieve highest reach and frequency possible in the target group.

Media Choice. For the first eight years Spot Radio dominated the spending. In 1977 this was supplemented with a small amount in Network Radio and Magazines. Network radio intended to supplement Spot coverage and also cover markets where there was no Spot advertising.

Vehicle Choice. For Spot Radio morning and afternoon radio drive time, housewife time, and on the weekend on Saturday 10:00 A.M. to 7 P.M. Network Radio to follow Spot time schedules.

Media Markets. By 1978 advertising was run in the nation's top forty-five markets, which accounted for 64% of the population.

Media Scheduling. Three flights per year with fairly equal spending: March–April, June–July, and November–December. Approximately 100 gross rating points per week.

V. OUTCOME

Panel studies in 1978 showed awareness of Stiller and Meara at 98% with strong identification of the couple with Blue Nun. Attitudes indicated no negatives. The brand was perceived as a high-quality, imported table wine for use on any occasion with any dish, meat or fish, and before or even after a meal. Sales of Blue Nun climbed from 68,000 cases in 1970 to approximately 1.2 million in 1978. Blue Nun became the number one selling premium white wine in the United States and the number three selling imported premium wine in the country.

American Egg Board Campaign

From 1977 to 1980, the American Egg Board increased its investment in network radio from 7% to 31%. Starting in January 1977, the media campaign developed by the American Egg Board's ad agency, Campbell-Mithun, had a budget of $3,600,000. The campaign was highly successful in both attracting consumers and winning awards. In October 1993, the American Egg Board campaign was awarded to Grey Advertising in New York, which, after an advertising hiautus, brought the egg back to radio.[2]

I. SITUATION ANALYSIS

The American Egg Board represents a commodity which, in 1980, accounted for $3.5 billion dollars in retail sales. Aside from occasional peaks and valleys, egg production had not increased since the mid-1940s despite substantial growth in the population. Prices, too, remained stable—the same in 1972 as in 1955. The industry was further plagued by dramatic swings in profitability as the egg producers that the American Egg Board represented were the victims of the market's erratic fluctuations.

Eggs were used in 95.6% of all U.S. households and were frequently described as one of "nature's most perfect foods." Eggs, high in quality protein, contain all of the amino acids and the vitamins known to exist, excluding C, plus thirteen minerals. Eggs are also one of the most versatile foods and can be scrambled, fried, boiled, baked, or poached. In addition, eggs are highly economical. A main dish of two eggs costs only about $0.15. A perceived product disadvantage, however, is the high cholesterol content of eggs, but at the time of this campaign the concern of high cholesterol and heart disease was not an important factor with most of the public. Despite all the advantages of eggs, per capita consumption declined from an annual total of 403 in 1945 to just 289 in 1974. From 1970 to 1974 alone, consumption dropped 22 eggs per person. After further declines in 1974, 1975, and 1976, an experimental test market campaign was launched in St. Louis with television, radio, and newspapers. Awareness and advertising results were impressive.

Consumer Research Indicated:

Changing life-styles with smaller and fewer breakfasts being consumed.
Cholesterol fears increasing, especially among older groups.
Increased competition from cold cereal, instant breakfasts, and egg substitutes.

Attitude Research Indicated:

Eggs have high-quality protein.
Eggs are among the most nutritious foods.
Eggs are low in calories.
Eggs and egg dishes are very good for snacks.
Eggs are a good value.
Eggs are good for all people.
Most people are generally aware of the positive values of eggs.

Market Segments Included:

Egg enthusiasts—feel positive toward eggs. Consume 39% more eggs per capita.
Breakfast skippers—like eggs but lack time.
Cholesterol avoiders—cut back on eggs because of cholesterol fears.
Egg dislikers—do not like the taste of eggs.
In 1978, 1979, and 1980 high beef prices led to "beef boycotts" and an increasing opportunity for a low-cost protein alternative.

II. ADVERTISING STRATEGY

Business Objective. Help reverse the decreasing per capita consumption of eggs.

Target. Heavy and medium users of eggs who tend to be homemakers, twenty-five to forty-nine years of age, located throughout the country is mostly A and B counties, with children at home between the ages of two and seventeen.

Positioning. As a natural choice for meals, snacks, appetizers, or any time of day. The American Egg Board wanted to appeal to egg enthusiasts, egg dislikers, cholesterol avoiders, and breakfast skippers.

Media Budget in 1977. $3,580,000.

Advertising Objective in 1977. To establish top-of-mind awareness and improve positive toward the egg since little positive news had been aired about eggs for years.

Media Budget in 1978. $3,619,000.

Advertising Objective in 1978. Shift to new uses for eggs and break out of the breakfast-only syndrome. Focus on price/value relationship of egg consumption.

> *Part 1.* Appeal to egg enthusiasts and breakfast skippers with non-breakfast uses.
> *Part 2.* Appeal to all four segments with general goodness, freshness, and naturalness story.

Media Budget in 1979. $3,400,000.

Advertising Objective in 1979. To continue to increase overall consumer attitudes toward eggs.

III. CREATIVE STRATEGY AND TACTICS

Primary Selling Point. Eggs are economical and incredible because they are versatile (any time of day, any number of ways).

Personality. A warm, friendly food that is incapable of being anything but useful and good.

1977. Emphasize egg's low calories, nutritional value, freshness, protein content, and versatility. The "Incredible Edible Egg" theme was introduced.

1978. Focus on new use and serving suggestions, eggs' ease and speed of preparation as well as their freshness, naturalness, nutrition, and versatility. Continue the "Incredible Edible Egg" theme. The public backlash against beef prices led to an egg strategy focusing on price/value benefits of eggs. Executed with six ads for radio.

1979. Continue with versatility, naturalness, and ease of preparation. Also, continue with price/value theme but expand into TV as well as radio.

1980. Focus on price/value on both radio and TV. Introduce new radio ads.

Creative Example

American Egg Board (thirty second)—Price/Value Theme
Theme music

HOMEMAKER: I used to complain a lot about the high cost of food. Now I'm doing something about it. Several times a week I serve an egg dish for lunch or dinner. The kids are crazy about egg sandwiches. I just scramble or fry an egg and serve it on a bun. You wouldn't believe what the kids put on them.

ANNOUNCER: Eggs are one of today's best food buys. For instance, when eggs cost 90 cents a dozen, they're only 60 cents a pound.

THEME MUSIC: The Incredible Edible Egg.

ANNOUNCER: The American Egg Board.

IV. MEDIA STRATEGY AND TACTICS

Early heavy use of TV with theme music and tag line always showing ways to prepare eggs.
Later increasing use of network radio emphasizing price/value and music giving strong repetition.

Magazines to give cooking ideas and recipes with visuals of egg-based foods.

1977 Media Strategy. Test heavy and light media schedules in four markets each: 7% network radio, 19% network TV, 59% spot TV, 15% magazines.

1978 Media Strategy. 8% network radio, 60% network TV, 28% spot TV, 4% magazines.

1979 Media Strategy. 13% network radio, 65% network TV, 22% magazines. Decreasing reliance on TV.

1980 Media Strategy. 31% network radio, 50% network TV, 19% magazines. A dramatic shift to radio with the price/value theme.

V. OUTCOME

Per capita and total egg consumption began rising in the fourth quarter of 1977 and continued through 1979. After twenty-two quarterly decreases, this was the most sustained increase since 1938. Attitude scores on seven key indicators increased significantly.

VI. UPDATES

From 1980 until 1985, the American Egg Board did very little advertising due to declining income. Because of its cost-efficiency, radio was the primary medium used during that time. From 1985 until late 1993, the American Egg Board changed its primary target to children and began advertising heavily on weekday syndicated after-school network TV programs and during weekday cartoon programs. However, in May 1993, Grey Advertising became the American Egg Board's new advertising-agency-of-record and put together an extensive advertising strategy. Utilizing an ad budget of $4.5 million, Grey devoted 16% to network radio, 30% to daytime network television, 43% to primetime network television, and 11% to national cable network television.

The 1993 to 1994 strategy was to reach the household decision makers, primarily women, when they would be most likely to buy or prepare eggs. Because market research studies have shown that most eggs are consumed during weekend breakfast, ads ran from Wednesday until Sunday, with radio the only medium running the spots during weekend mornings. These radio ads became the last message the household decision maker heard before cracking an egg in the skillet. Creatively, "The Incredible Edible Egg" was still utilized as the tagline for each thirty-second radio network spot, but the campaign took on a new flavor under the theme "I Love Eggs."

Nutri/System—Canada[3]

I. SITUATION ANALYSIS

A. Product Analysis. Nutri/System, a weight loss franchise launched in the United States in 1971, was created to meet the demands of an appearance-conscious and time-restricted society. The diet centers help individuals lose weight by controling calorie intake through use of the foods created by Nutri/System. Individuals purchase the food products and follow the dietary guidelines to achieve their desired weight reduction.

The foods, available only at Nutri/System locations, come in a variety of forms including boil-in-a-bag, oven/microwave ready, or instant. Dieters select their foods at each weekly visit with a nutritionist. The Nutri/System diet is very close to that of The Diabetes Association, with low sodium and low fat. The Nutri/System package designs illustrate exact portions and suggest servings without embellishments. The premise behind Nutri/System is that people can actually eat a large amount of healthy, low fat foods to lose weight and feel good.

B. Customer Analysis. When Nutri/System opened in 1971, a major change was taking place across the United States and Canada with the beginning of a health and exercise phenomena. People were becoming very physically active to achieve optimum appearance. "Working out" became a popular daily activity and aerobics was starting to make a big impact. While nearly everyone bought a fitness club membership to lose weight, not everyone enjoyed it or even used it. For those who didn't like to exercise, Nutri/System offered a weight-loss solution. One characteristic of many Nutri/System users is that they tend to be procrastinators, making time an important factor. With this in mind, Nutri/System made all discount prices available for a limited time in order to create urgency among the public. Nutri/System customers generally fall in the lower-middle to upper-middle classes.

C. Competitive and Market Analysis. In 1971, Weight Watchers was the only other major player in the weight loss industry. However, Weight Watchers was an entirely different type of weight loss center, so was not considered heavy competition to Nutri/System. No other weight-loss center offered Nutri/System's diet and prepared foods. Weight Watchers' diet program consisted of measuring and weighing food portions as well as attending meetings to discuss weight problems. Nutri/System, on the other hand, offered appropriate food portions with no fuss, and meetings were held only with a nutritionist who encouraged and supported the dieter.

The 1992 emergence of Jenny Craig created competition for Nutri/System.

II. ADVERTISING STRATEGY

A. Advertising Objective. To establish Nutri/System as the easiest and most effective way to lose weight and keep it off. This concept was illustrated by well-known radio personnel who participated in the Nutri/System program.

Marketing Objective. To increase penetration in Canadian

markets. To establish Nutri/System as *the* choice for the weight-conscious consumer.

Target Market. Adults 24+, with a heavy skew of 90% to 95% female.

B. Positioning. Nutri/System is an easy and effective way to lose weight and keep it off.

C. Media Advertising Budget. From 1986 through 1991, the entire weight loss industry had an average advertising budget in the tens of millions of dollars with heavy concentration in radio, print, and television.

Rollout. The move into Canada began in 1986. Advertising started in Toronto, and rapidly spread from Victoria, British Columbia to St. John's, Newfoundland in just five years. The majority of Nutri/System locations were franchised, and advertising rollout followed accordingly. A total of 306 locations were established throughout Canada from 1986 to 1991.

III. CREATIVE STRATEGY AND TACTICS

A. Copy Platform / Creative Objective. To convey the ease of the Nutri/System diet program. To illustrate that anyone can effectively lose weight and keep it off with Nutri/System. To create a sense of urgency through limited-time offers to consumers.

Tactics. Nutri/System wanted to use radio in Canada from the start of its 1986 introduction but Consumer and Corporate Affairs (CCA) considered it a food product and insisted it have a broadcast number, which would entail a lengthy registration procedure with the government. Nutri/System in the United States had been working on "DJ Radio," where someone at a radio station was on the Nutri/System program and often the announcer or another staff member would interact with the dieter. With Nutri/System's DJ Radio, there is little or no mention of the food, as the live radio spots discuss the dieter's success with the entire Nutri/System program. Nutri/System in Canada approached the CCA to sell DJ Radio which utilized an emotion factor rather than advertising the actual food products. The CCA approved this concept so Nutri/System was able to begin this same type of radio advertising.

The station announcers or other station personnel who participated in the program actually lost weight and kept it off. Pre-recorded commercial material was taken from the testimonials of the individuals on the program. Special discount prices were offered during live, on-air interviews with Nutri/System representatives who emphasized the urgency of the discount offer. All other recorded radio spots also included some type of discount price special.

B. Develop Ad Executions.

Format. Three different styles of commercials were produced—prerecorded on tape where the individual used a script to discuss his or her weight loss and emphasize the Nutri/System special price offer; live on tape where the individual would talk about the program without the use of a script; and live on-air, or quick response, where a Nutri/System representative would be present during the announcer's show to talk about the program and discuss a special offer to radio listeners who immediately called the station.

Slogan. Lose all the weight you want and keep it off.

Creative Example. A live, on-tape testimonial by an announcer who participated in the Nutri/System weight loss program:

ANNOUNCER: Hi, Ken Packman here for Nutri/System. Now the first two words you just heard are probably the most important. Nutri system. It's a great system that works and one you can live with for the long haul. Hey, we all pick up a little baggage we don't need . . . before you know it, you hop on the scale, and . . . ohhh, boy! Sure makes you take a deep breath doesn't it? Especially after you've enjoyed all those great things all through the Christmas and holiday season. Well, I got news for you, they got a heck of a deal right now, and all you have to do is call 1–800–321-THIN, and find out how you can lose all your weight and pay only a dollar per pound for each pound you have to lose. Nutri/System foods additional, certain conditions apply. Simply call Nutri/System now, and lose all your weight for only a dollar a pound. It's that simple. Now does it work you say? "Oh, I've heard all the stories about this, that, and the other." Nutri/System is not this, that, and the other. I've lost 40 pounds on Nutri/System. Give them a call right now. 1–800–321-THIN! Nutri/System . . . it works!

IV. MEDIA STRATEGY AND TACTICS

A. Media Objectives and Goals. To reach Canadians in every market through heavy use of media. To be recognized as *the* weight loss center in Canada.

B. Inter- and Intra- Media Decisions.

Media Choice. The 1986 through 1991 media mix included radio, television, and print. Nutri/System ran on every radio station across Canada, English and French, where they allowed testimonial advertising. Local and regional newspapers took care of the print buy, and national television advertising completed the media campaign.

Vehicle Choice. Mondays, Tuesdays, and either Wednesdays or Sundays were purchased for radio, print, and television. All broadcast dayparts were bought with an 8:00 P.M. cut-off time. Many radio announcers were on the Nutri/System diet so the advertising schedules centered around their shows.

Media Markets. Advertising ran in both large and small markets in over 300 centers in English and French Canada, wherever there was a Nutri/System location. More than 75% of the population was reached with the message.

Media Scheduling. Fifty-two weeks were purchased, with the December weight moved to January.

V. OUTCOME

Through the use of heavy radio, print, and television, Nutri/System established itself as the number one choice for weight reduction throughout Canada. The advertising support in large and small markets aided the penetration, awareness, and the urgency required to successfully position Nutri/System as the leader.

Radio played a very significant role in Nutri/System's success. According to Murray Smith, Advisor in Image Marketing & Advertising for Profile Marketing, Nutri/System's advertising consulting firm which places all media, "Radio drove leads phenomenally. The average number of calls in a market when using the radio quick response increased by 300%. The quick response was bought at nearly every station. Advertising in the weight loss industry is critical—you have to be there. The results were phenomenal, radio turned our business around. When we first started advertising on radio, the leads in some markets doubled. We credit all the penetration and success to radio."

Case Example Summaries

The case examples serve several purposes. First, they highlight the general format of the campaign plan—the centerpiece document for most modern advertising work. Though these plans are retrospective and include less detail than is required to document a campaign plan, they help illustrate the issues that need treatment in the plan.

These examples also illustrate the divergent roles that radio can serve in a media plan. Blue Nun was a product that did not demand illustration. The brand was small and could not support massive advertising. Furthermore, the wine market was expanding and Blue Nun required an affordable advertising medium that provided flexibility for their geographic coverage. For the first eight years spot radio dominated the media mix almost exclusively, and spot radio purchases expanded from three to forty-five markets over this time. Gradually, as distribution expanded, the economics of network radio plus its ability to fill in the holes left by spot market coverage dictated that it become a part of the media mix. As indicated by the strong awareness and attitude scores, the strategy of using radio almost exclusively worked for this brand.

For the American Egg Board, the initial need was a national campaign that could illustrate the multiple uses of eggs. For the first several years, network television advertising and magazines dominated the media strategy because of their ability to tangibly illustrate appetizing alternative preparation of eggs. With a competitive opportunity to emphasize the economics of eggs against the skyrocketing price of meat came the chance for radio to excel. Tests of a price/value theme on radio were extremely successful. Suddenly, being visual wasn't as important as communicating to people's wallets, and media prices were rising faster than the advertising budget. Radio was seen as an economical alternative to television. The shift from 8% to 31% of the budget for network radio was a result of the medium's proven performance of the price/value theme and its ability to maintain repetition with an affordable budget. No spot radio was used because the American Egg Board's supporting constituency of producers is spread throughout the United States. In 1993, radio, once again, became a dominant advertising medium due to its cost-efficiency and its ability to reach the primary target during weekend mornings—the time when decision makers are most likely to purchase, prepare, and consume eggs.

From the moment Nutri/System began advertising on hundreds of radio stations across Canada in 1986, awareness of the weight loss centers and of their special offers and programs skyrocketed. Via live on-air, live taped, and pre-recorded scripted commercials, Nutri/System utilized an emotional factor to reach consumers and spread the word of its effective programs. Radio personalities and their co-workers started their own Nutri/System diets and encouraged radio listeners to join them. The live and pre-recorded testimonial radio campaign was so successful that Nutri/System's advertising consulting firm attributes radio alone with a 300% increase in consumer responses to certain Nutri/System specials.

A Critical Process

The campaign planning process is critical and helps identify the need for media choices that consider the product needs, budget, competition, distribution patterns, message needs, audience lifestyle, exposure, and virtually every aspect examined in an advertising campaign analysis. Radio is an enormously flexible medium that can play a major role for many different products and in many situations. It has been neglected by many advertisers who have either ignored it completely or given it only token treatment in their media plans.

Chapter 4
Getting Specific: Finding Patterns in the Sand

It's not so much what we know that hurts us, it's what we think we know that ain't so.

—Will Rodgers

Despite having nearly 70 years of experience with radio advertising, our knowledge about what makes an ad successful remains largely a mystery among most advertising practitioners and academics.[1,2] The following chapters take a major step toward explaining the techniques that are used most often and most successfully in radio advertising. This chapter starts with a brief look at what recent TV and radio research tells us about developing advertising.

Recent Broadcast Research

A number of generalizations emerged from recent television research[3] of over 1,000 pretested commercials:

1. Product category plays an important role in determining what works and what does not work in advertising messages.
2. The most important message factor is the presence of a brand-differentiating aspect.
3. Recall and persuasion is accounted for by two sets of ele-

ments: brand performance characteristics, such as brand-differentiating claims and convenience of the product in use, and attention and memory factors, such as humor, auditory memory devices, brand prominence in the commercial, front-end impact, and brand sign-off.

4. Factors that appear to harm recall and comprehension are: company identification, information about product attributes and components, and information on nutrition and health.

In another relatively recent TV study partially reported in Oglivy and Raphaelson[4] other variables emerge. The research, which was privately commissioned, studied 809 TV commercials for food, appliances, apparel, and five other products that are not identified. Ads that scored above average in persuasion had the following features: .

1. Problem/solution format
2. Pertinent humor
3. Advertising-developed characters or personalities who become associated with the brand
4. Slice-of-life with a doubter converted
5. Newness (new product, new uses, new ideas, new information)
6. Candid camera testimonials
7. Demonstrations

This recent study confirms earlier proprietary TV studies[5] done at Burke and McCollum/Spielman that also found that product category accounts for a substantial variance in the performance of ad elements. In addition, these television studies conclude that advertising structure and style do appear to have a substantial impact on TV ad performance. Not coincidentally, as detailed later in this chapter, the research reported in the remainder of this book takes into account product category variation and also looks at the specific impact of message structure and style on radio ad performance.

Radio Research

Radio advertising research provides only limited insight for constructing good ads because like most TV studies, it understands the importance of product category variations but does not directly consider the effect of product category. Instead the literature is dominated by general prescriptions. Some give rules to remember, such as use attention getters, zero in on the audience, keep it simple, sell early and often, write for the ear, and mention the client often.

In this book *How to Make Your Advertising Make Money,* John Caples[6] proclaimed for retail ads that typewritten commercials read by a station announcer were best and that the best ads did not entertain, had no jingles, no humor, just 100% persuasion. Book, Car, and Tannenbaum[7] distilled their own similar list: write for the ear, capture and excite the listener's imagination, stick to one strong idea, single out your prospect, set the mood for your prospect, remember mnemonics and get attention fast, register the products's name, don't overwrite, make your appeal clear, if it's news, make it sound important, multiply TV (use TV soundtracks), keep a friendly feeling going, be sure your humorous spots are funny, give the reader something to do, and once is not enough.

Though these prescriptions might be comforting, the absence of possible product category differences brings into question the domain of products to which these findings relate. For instance, do these results apply equally to insurance ads, snack foods, fashion clothing, and beer? Sewall and Sarel[8] concluded from a large radio study that the impact of executional message variables varies substantially by product category. Their result calls into further question the usefulness of broad prescriptions that do not consider product category differences.

What is clear is that very little is known about what works in radio advertising. What we think we know may be so general without considering product categories that it is of little value in constructing radio ads.

Developing Radio Messages: A Situational Approach

A useful framework that does consider the product category is found in the work of consumer researchers Richard Petty and John Cacciopo[9] in their Elaboration Likelihood Motel (ELM). Their ELM approach is that the advertising message should be adjusted according to whether consumers have low or high motivation and/or ability to process an ad that they see or hear. A low motivation situation might be for a routinely purchased packaged goods where there is little need or desire by consumers to focus on the advertising message. Here it would be unnecessary or unwise to focus exclusively on product messages to communicate. This differs sharply from the new product or non-routine purchase where there is higher motivation by consumers to process message-related information in ads. When the audience has low motivation/ability, for instance when they are buying toothpaste or soft drinks, peripheral message cues in an ad have greater influence on consumers than if motivation/ability is high when they are shopping for a major appliance or insurance. Peripheral cues include music, humor, mnemonics, presenters, and other elements that do not convey the message directly, but serve to capture the attention of a consumer unmotivated to focus on purely informational ads. These elements are secondary or peripheral to the main message even though they may be closely tied to the message. Central cues are the main selling points of the product and are more important when there is high motivation/ability by consumers to process ad messages. With central processing the quality of message arguments is more important than the quantity of arguments. Petty and Cacciopo have demonstrated that peripheral cues are more effective in situations when there is low ability/motivation to process information and central message cues are effective when consumers are motivated and have the ability to process messages.

The lesson for radio advertising and any other advertising medium is that the advertising team needs to acknowledge the different consumer desire for information in order to develop effective ad messages.

This chapter and those that follow reveal how radio ad executions vary by product and the consumer's motivation to listen to radio messages. Of course, there are sometimes differences in the motivation of different consumers toward the same products. However, this approach of grouping products to capture similar motivations toward processing advertising messages does address the degree to which the majority of consumers are motivated to be involved and thoughtful toward products and ad messages. To this extent the results are far more accurate than treating all products as the same when developing prescriptions for advertising messages. What is clear is that the nature of the product must be considered and that the principles of the ELM model must be brought into the equation. While prior work tells us that style and structural aspects of ads such as music, humor, format, length, number of ideas, and numerous other devices can play a major role in predicting advertising success, additional work in radio is needed to focus these findings on relatively homogenous sets of products.

A Product Color Matrix

To address the product issue more directly than in the past this study specifically incorporates product categories before starting the analysis (see Figure 4–1). This does not mean that each product is treated uniquely, nor does it mean all consumers approach the same product in the same way. There are patterns of behavior that consumers fall into when purchasing products. The marketing idea of grouping products into similar clusters is, of course, not new—every student of marketing is familiar with the convenience, shopping, specialty, and unsought categories used in textbooks for decades. Some products are obtained mainly for their functionality and involve a dominance of thought or basic needs (business products, insurance, appliances) over emotion or wants (perfume, snacks, fashion clothing). Similarly, some goods and services are more durable and expensive, involving high risk, while others involve low risk and are purchased on a routine basis.

	Functional Tools	Expressive Toys
Higher Risk	**WHITE Goods** *Bigger Tools* Large appliances Business equipment Insurance Auto tires Etc.	**RED Goods** *Bigger Toys* Fashion clothing and accessories Hair coloring Motorcycle Sports car Fashion luggage Jewelry Etc.
Lower Risk	**BLUE Goods** *Little Tools* Detergents and household cleaners OTC remedies Motor oil and gas Most non-dessert foods	**YELLOW Goods** *Little Toys & Treats* Snack foods Desserts Beer Alcohol Tobacco products

Figure 4–1

The Product Color Matrix (PCM)
Consumer Objective

Though these variations in purchasing are well known, limitations in the size and product variation of the data sets available to earlier researchers restricted the type of analysis they could conduct. For this book there was a data set large enough to subdivide products before the analysis began according to the product clusters from the Product Color Matrix (see Figure 4–1). A separate analysis was conducted on each of the four Color Matrix product sets, allowing for better insight about the elements of good and bad radio ads at a more homogeneous product level than in the past. The advantage is that this research explicitly recognizes the differences in products and then conducts analysis to give unique insight to each product group.

The basis for the Product Color Matrix used here is research conducted in consumer behavior and later applied at Foote, Cone, and Belding,[10] at DDB Needham Worldwide,[11] and by other researchers including Rossiter, Percy, and Donovan.[12] Each developed product or decision-making classifications sim-

ilar to the ELM model that build in a recognition of the involvement consumers have with the products. A variation of these
earlier approaches is developed here to provide a framework for
the analysis in this chapter and of successful and unsuccessful
radio ads that is presented in the remainder of the book.

Tools Versus Toys

The Product Color Matrix is presented here to highlight the differences between products that need to be considered when developing advertising. The principles come from the ELM idea of
the willingness and ability of audiences to deal with information. Along one dimension of the Color Matrix is a "Tools"
versus "Toys" breakdown and along the other is a "Low" versus "High" Risk dimension. For products in the Low Risk dimension, involvement is lower because many decisions are routine and the products are at a lower cost. In the ELM
framework these are products for which audiences will have a
lower motivation or need to process information. Along the
"Tool" side of the "Tools and Toys" dimension are products
that fill more logical or functional needs instead of products
that reward and fill more expressive needs. WHITE products in
the Color Matrix exemplify the Big Tool products.

WHITE Goods

Using the Product Color Matrix, WHITE products are high-
risk, expensive purchases and often fill a functional need. Items
such as refrigerators, washer/dryers, and other large appliances
are the products that retailers traditionally have called "WHITE
goods." They are durable and expensive requiring consumers to
shop and compare because of the risk involved with the choice.
Of course other products, such as insurance, non-sport automo-
biles, and many non-routine business products, are also among
the products in this cell. From an advertising perspective, consumers evaluating these WHITE products should be motivated
to use more central, message-related cues than ads for products

in other less risky and less tool-oriented Product Color Matrix cells.

RED Goods

The second cell of the Product Color Matrix consists of what are labeled RED products. Red is chosen because it symbolizes flamboyance and is expressive like the products that are represented here. The sports car, the motorcycle, the red dress, fancy tie, or jewelry that represent the individual and have high risk are the RED goods. The WHITE and RED goods have high risk in common. However, for the WHITE goods the high risk might be dominated by significant financial risk while for the with RED products there is as likely to be social risk as well as financial risk. WHITE goods are Big Tools while RED goods are Big Toys. While WHITE goods satisfy a functional goal, RED goods help satisfy the more conspicuous and flamboyant goals that the expressive sports car or designer fashion clothes appeal to. The radio advertising for WHITE and RED products should be different to match the different motivations evoked by the products.

BLUE Goods

The third cell of the Product Color Matrix is BLUE and represents low risk and functional decision making. Products in this group are "Little Tools" that are consumable and help accomplish small but essential tasks like cleaning, cooking, and personal hygiene. BLUE goods include mouthwash, toilet bowl cleaner, and laundry detergent that are part of this set of routinely made purchases. Staple food items, many health and beauty aids, and over-the-counter drugs all fall into this grouping. As they are low-risk and functional products, there is less willingness or need by consumers to process information than for the more risky WHITE goods, but because there is a functional or tool aspect to the products, there is some interest in relevant information. There should be a mix of central message-oriented and peripheral message cues in ads in this group of products reflecting the functional but low-risk aspect of the products.

YELLOW Goods

Finally, there are the YELLOW goods that are the "Little Toys or Treats" that are the day-to-day rewards. Snack chips and beer are the most appropriate color metaphors for the YEL-LOW goods, but the list would include other products such as gum, candy, soft drinks, and cigarettes. These products are the low-risk, routine purchases that help make us feel a little better, but they are not as important as the RED goods, which also satisfy wants and are expressive. The ELM framework would classify this product group into a low motivation to process category because of the low risk and routine nature of the decision making. The need or desire for consumers to process message-related information about these YELLOW products should be low.

Through its four cells, the Product Color Matrix provides metaphors for the psychology behind how consumers act toward products in each category. All of the analyses conducted in the remainder of this book use the Product Color Matrix approach to group products before trying to understand the patterns of radio advertising construction that have been used, and which ones work and which ones fail.

The Product Color Matrix in This Radio Study

More than 2,000 pretested ads were classified into one of four of the Color Matrix cells. The products were grouped in the most appropriate of the four color cells (Table 4–1). The result yielded between 192 and 731 ads for each cell of the Product Color Matrix. To maintain strict confidentiality, company or brand names could not be mentioned in any of the discussions and analyses in this book. The radio case studies used to illustrate products found in each of the four product color groups

Table 4-1

Products Represented in this Study—
Product Color Matrix Groups

White (317)	Red (192)	Blue (708)	Yellow (731)
Business services	Jeans	Prepared foods	Candy bars
Business	Grooming aids	Cold medicine	Sodas
machines	Sportswear	Paint, hardware	Wine
Cars	Hair coloring	Stomach remedy	Chewing gums
Insurance		Gas, oil	Coffee
Banking		Vitamins	Snack foods
Trucks		Other medicine	Hard candy
		Cereal	Beers
		Deodorant	
		Analgesics	
		Cleaners	
		Feminine hygiene	
		Toothpaste	
		Mouthwash	
		Other clothes	
		Antiseptic	
		Bleach	
		Detergents	

Numbers in parentheses indicate sample size.

are not necessarily part of the study but are used only to provide the reader with a clearer understanding of how specific creative elements work within each product category.

What Devices Do Radio Advertisers Use?

The starting point for examining 2,000 radio ads was to identify the range of executional characteristics and devices used in radio ads. We found over three dozen characteristics that fall into one of three broad headings: Message Style, Message Structure, or Presenter (see Tables 2–2a and 2–2b and Appendix B). These commercial characteristics were screened from the larger body of data developed in over fifteen years of testing by Radio Recall Research, Inc. (see Appendixes A and B).

In Tables 4–2a and 4–2b the variety of executional options among the 2,000 commercials becomes evident. We have displayed by product color group the frequency of use of all of the executional features coded into the ad files. These two tables by themselves provide a unique profile of the use each of the commercial features has had in this very large sample of radio ads. The results broken down in the Color Matrix product grouping tell us the most and least popular executional tactics in radio.

The importance of using the Product Color Matrix analysis can be seen in the variation in the profile of commercial features across the color groups. Under the *Message Style* (see Table 4–2a) there are some characteristics that were used quite similarly across the Product Color Matrix. For example, Something New (new product, improvement, new package, new use or hoopla) was used quite uniformly in 15.1% to 19.6% of ads. Most of the radio ads do not state something new but reiterate what has been said before. However, in the Humor and Music category there is much more variation in the Product Color Matrix. In the lower risk BLUE and YELLOW products much more humor was used than with the WHITE or RED products. The ads for YELLOW goods used humor in more than 40% of all ads while the ads for RED goods used it just 11% of the time. The implication is that WHITE and RED products with their higher risk are seen by creatives as less amenable to the use of humor than are the lower-risk YELLOW and BLUE products. Similarly, the mix of Music varies sharply across Product Color Matrix cells. For Music the more expressive RED and YELLOW goods use music of some form in at least three of four ads with especially heavy use of jingles. The use of Mnemonics ranged from a low of 42% for BLUE goods to a high of 60% for WHITE goods. For all product groups, when mnemonics were used, functional mnemonics were employed in more than nine out of ten ads.

In the *Message Structure* variables in Table 4–2b the mix of formats, as expected, varies markedly. The very traditional Announcer format is dominant in use for all product cells, but even

Table 4–2a
Message Style in the Color Matrix

Message Style	White (%)	Red (%)	Blue (%)	Yellow (%)
Something New	15.1	15.1	18.0	19.6
Humor				
No Humor	85.9	89.0	64.6	58.9
Related Humor	7.7	8.9	22.0	23.0
Unrelated Humor	6.4	2.1	13.4	18.1
Music				
No Music	48.3	16.1	40.6	23.4
Jingles	7.3	43.2	12.2	28.3
Singing Music	4.4	16.7	9.5	19.4
Other Music	40.1	24.0	37.8	28.8
Audio				
Related Audio	68.8	83.9	72.2	77.4
Unrelated Audio	31.2	16.1	27.8	22.6
Origin				
TV Sound	—	—	—	—
TV Version	6.3	—	3.5	7.6
Radio Sound	93.7	100	96.5	92.4
Mnemonics				
No Mnemonics	39.7	46.6	58.2	50.6
Functional	58.4	50.3	37.1	46.0
Non-functional	1.9	3.1	4.7	3.4
Fantasy	—	—	—	—

All ads included in sample.

its usage changes from 41.6% of ads in the WHITE Cell to an astonishing 83.9% of ads in the RED Cell. The Testimonial format is used relatively little with the exception of WHITE goods. Ads for WHITE goods had the most diverse use of formats, frequently employing Announcer, Testimonial, Slice of Life, Interview, and Problem Solution formats. For the lower-risk BLUE and YELLOW goods, after the dominant Announcer format, Slice of Life was used in at least one of four ads. Even the use of sixty-second ads varied from 60.3% for WHITE products down to just 19.5% for BLUE products (see Table 4–2b).

In the *Presenter* category of variables the use of Male pre-

Table 4-2b
Message Structure in the Color Matrix

	White	Red	Blue	Yellow
Message Structure				
Testimonial	17.0%	2.6%	7.0%	6.5%
Interview	13.9%	1.6%	1.7%	1.0%
Slice of Life	15.5%	2.6%	24.8%	29.2%
Problem Solution	12.0%	7.3%	2.0%	1.0%
Demonstration	0%	2.1%	2.0%	1.8%
Announcer	41.6%	83.9%	62.5%	61.0%
60" Length	60.3%	52.6%	19	38.6%
# Words	134	101	94	103.3%
Entry Time	9	8	9	8.3%
# Brand Mentions	6	6	4	5.3%
# Ideas	6	4	4	4.3%
# Message Repetitions	3	3	3	3.3%
Presenter				
# Presenters	3	2	2.3	3
Male	63.7	50.8%	59.3%	58.0%
Female	0%	18.8%	9.6%	7.3%
Both Together	36.3	30.4%	31.1%	34.7%
Adult	97.8	98.4%	94.2%	92.3%
Teen	1.3	1.6%	1.1%	4.3%
Mixed Adult and Other	.9	0%	4.7%	3.4%

senters dominated each of the product groups. Female presenters were used relatively little from 0% for WHITE products to just 18.8% for RED products. Perhaps this is because women have just recently begun to become a dominant presence in radio commercials. In other words, men had, historically, been the sole spokespersons for some advertisers for so long that they have only started expanding their horizons to include women. Though women were used in about one of three ads with men, the negligible use of women alone as presenters is extremely surprising especially given the high percentage of food and other non-durables in the BLUE and YELLOW goods categories.

An Ad Profile: WHITE Goods

As WHITE goods are high-risk and tool-oriented products, it is expected that most ads in this category would focus on substance rather than form. This fact is supported in that just 14.1% of ads attempt humor, about half use music, with only 7.3% employing jingles. Generally the ads in this group are longer, use more words, and include more brand mentions and ideas than ads in the other cells of the Product Color Matrix. Presenters in this group are always either men or men with women, never women by themselves.

An Ad Profile: RED Goods

RED goods like WHITE goods are high in risk, but they are more expressive than WHITE goods. Humor is used here even less than for WHITE goods. On the other hand, music is used in 83.9% of RED cell ads with jingles in 43.2%. Perhaps music is seen as a vehicle to convey the expressive emotions in this category. Surprisingly, the Announcer format is dominant for the RED goods with negligible use of the flexible Slice of Life format. The greatest use of women presenting alone is found in this product group though even at 18.8% women are used far less than male presenters.

An Ad Profile: BLUE Goods

BLUE goods satisfy our daily basic needs, so some consumers need some information but are generally unmotivated to attend to these ads. Humor is used in 35.4% of these ads and usually the humor is related to the product. Music is used in 59.4% of the ads but jingles are not very common. Mnemonics are used in 41.8% of ads, an amount that is lower than for the other product groups. The Announcer and Slice of Life formats are found in 62.5% and 24.8% of ads, respectively. Surprisingly 80% of the ads for these BLUE products are less than sixty seconds long and they tend to have fewer words and fewer brand mentions. The presenters are dominated by men with just under 10% of ads using women alone as presenters.

An Ad Profile: YELLOW Goods

These products represent the low-risk treats that life offers us on a day-to-day basis. The most humor is used here (41.1%), as well as a great deal of music (76.6%) with frequent jingles and singing. Mnemonics are used on a par with other product groups in about 50% of ads. The Announcer format and Slice of Life are again the most common, as found with the BLUE goods. As for the BLUE goods, the ads tend to be less than sixty seconds long and are, again, largely dominated by male presenters.

All of these variations in commercial features would be obscured with a typical analysis that did not consider the importance of product differences throughout the research. This information is interesting because it tells us what techniques are used by many radio advertisers. In addition to knowing what creative techniques are "hot" and prevalent, advertisers and their agencies need to know what is effective. To answer that question we need to examine the success of these ads. This important question is considered in the succeeding chapters. Before doing that, however, we will briefly explore the measures used in the data set to determine the success or failure of the radio ads discussed.

How Do We Know if a Radio Ad Works?

The debate about how to judge whether an ad is good or bad has raged among advertising people for a long time. To help settle the dispute about which measures of ad effectiveness work the best, the Advertising Research Foundation (ARF) embarked on a Copy Research Validity Project in 1982. The project pitted alternative recall, communication, persuasion, liking, and diagnostic measures against one another to predict actual product sales in split-cable market environments. The result is a landmark study by Russell Haley[13] which cut through much of the partisan rhetoric and provides tangible evidence. The results are important for this book because Haley's report supports the use of pretesting in general and with a mix of dependent variables as were used in this book. For each category of dependent variables, there was a correlation with sales, but with some measures performing better than others. The results suggest that a battery of different recall, liking, and persuasion measures are individually correlated with sales effects. The most reliable approach is a blend of different measurements. The outcome of the ARF study is a highly credible vindication of quantitative advertising commercial testing. In particular, former critics of recall tests must now acknowledge that some traditional recall tests that actually measure attention, communication and, comprehension/communication are highly predictive of actual product sales. The evidence is quite compelling for the low-involvement products, a group for which recall measures have been particularly criticized. Based on Haley's ARF work, persuasion, a measure many have thought most predictive of sales, it generally less predictive than the better recall, communication, liking, and comprehension measures.

In fact, it is the rare advertising testing firm that employs just one measure. As the debate between those advocating recall versus persuasion faded, it had become clear even before the recent ARF study that a combination of measures is desirable and that these measures should be used with extreme care.

As Haley's work suggests, this book utilizes a blend of measures that together provide more reliability than any one measure of advertising success. Recall was the earliest measure of advertising used by market research firms, but of course, recall means different things to different researchers and in the data set that is used for this book there were six different measures of recall (see Appendix A for more detail):

1. Unaided Brand Recall
2. Category-Aided Recall
3. Claimed (brand-aided) Recall

4. Proven Recall
5. Message Recall
6. Execution Recall

These six measures represent an array of remembering related and unrelated to the product, and with or without prompting. In fact, in relation to the ARF study, these six so-called recall measures are really a blend of recall, communication, and comprehension. The first three of the above six measures correspond to three recall measures tested by ARF. Of the three, the first, Unaided Brand Recall, outperformed the others and was able to predict sales 87% of the time in the ARF study!

Items 4, 5, and 6 above correspond to the measures labeled communication in the ARF study. Of the three, Proven Recall (main point communication) and Execution Recall (ad situation/visual) performed particularly well. Recall of key copy points—Message Recall—has even been granted the status of a "comprehension" rather than a recall measure by some researchers.[14]

In this book the first five recall measures listed above above were most highly intercorrelated (Cronbach's alpha of .93). When a composite index of the first five recall variables was developed, the individual item correlation ranged from .86 (brand recall) to .93 (claimed recall). The creation of this "Communication Index" out of the five individual measures was designed to provide a more reliable indicator of the recall/communication/comprehension construct than any one variable by itself could provide. Execution Recall correlated in the .6 to .7 range with the other recall variables and it was used as a separate measure of ad performance. Proven Recall, though also part of the Communication Index, is reported separately because of its high regard by practitioners and the positive correlation with sales found in the ARF study.

Persuasion is a variable created in this study by subtracting the pre-exposure purchase intention expressed by consumers from their post radio ad exposure purchase intention scores. Both measures were obtained from respondents before they left the mall setting where audiences were exposed to the radio ads (see Appendix A). Persuasion here refers to the change in purchase intent as expressed as a percentage from 0 to 100. The range of persuasion for the whole sample is from −65% to + 62% with a mean of 2.5%. This means that some consumers' purchase intentions rose and some declined after they heard the radio ads.

The combination of the Communication Index, Proven Recall, Execution Recall, and Persuasion provides a credible array of ways to evaluate the success of the 2,000 radio ads in the sample. In the remaining chapters the value of *Message Structure, Message Style,* and *Presenter* elements are examined using these dependent measures of success.

Table 4–3
Summary of Dependent Measures in this Study

Communication Index- alpha .93 among measures
This index combines the recall scores from each of the following five items into a single performance measure that is more reliable than any one score by itself.
Unaided Brand Recall
Category Aided Recall
Claimed (brand-aided) Recall
Proven Recall—labeled a communication measure by ARF Study
Message Recall—labeled a comprehension measure by ARF Study

Communication—Proven Recall
This variable is part of the Communication Index but is also broken out separately here. It is historically used widely in the industry and a similar measure was highly correlated with sales in the ARF Study.

Communication—Execution Recall
This is the one variable that was not part of the Communication Index but is a good predictor of sales based on the ARF Study.

Persuasion
This measure was calculated, but based on the ARF Study, is not likely to be as good a predictor of sales as the other variables.

For more details about the measures, see Appendices A and C.

Chapter Summary

The most useful way to study radio advertising is by looking first at product category groupings. The ELM theory of tailoring messages to the motivation levels of consumers to process information in the message was used as an underlying theme to develop the Product Color Matrix. Dividing products into WHITE, RED, BLUE, and YELLOW clusters captures the consumer's motivation to process different types of advertising information. The color theme reflects the Tool versus Toy and High versus Low Risk nature of the products. Ads in each color group are rich in their use of varied executional style, structure, and presenter devices.

The multiple measures of commercial effectiveness (Communication Index, Proven Recall, Execution Recall, and Persuasion) are important to obtain a true evaluation of ad effectiveness. By analyzing the various Message Structure, Style, and Presenter elements in each color cluster, and looking for patterns among the ineffective ads and the successful ones, we'll see what works and what doesn't.

Chapter 5

Anatomy of a Good Commercial for High-Risk Tools—WHITE Cell Products

Failure is the foundation of success, and the means by which it is achieved. Success is the lurking-place of failure; but who can tell when the turning point will come?

—Lao-Tse

C reators of radio commercials have a number of components available to them when structuring an advertisement. Most, if not all, of these elements fall into one of three creative categories: message style, message structure, and presenter characteristics. To develop effective advertisements, it is necessary to be able to predict when each of these creative elements will or will not work. Information identifying the potential impact of these elements is crucial to those involved in the development of radio commercials. This, and the next chapters, analyze those creative elements that make up a radio commercial and identify those which lead to effective advertisements.

A straightforward and convenient way to approach this analysis is from the perspective of the product. To do this, each radio commercial in the study was grouped into the four color-coded product classifications identified in the previous chapter. Then, each creative element was examined to determine whether it had a positive or negative effect on the commercial's performance. The success rate—determined by whether a commercial that had high recall and persuasion scores contained the element—was then calculated for each creative element. Conversely, since it is also important to know what doesn't work, the presence of each creative element was also measured for poor commercials.

The goal of this inquiry is not to lay down hard-and-fast rules as to what does or does not work, but to give an indication of which characteristics are associated with good and poor radio commercials. Knowing "the odds" of what works best for certain types of products will allow copywriters to develop better and more effective radio copy. Of course, there may be times when "going against the odds" is the best strategy. This becomes a judgment call for the copywriter, but better decisions are made when the odds are known. One basic, yet crucial, element to keep in mind when writing radio commercials is that, regardless of the product category, the sound and tone of each spot should match the radio format where it will be heard. For example, a loud, boisterous ad for a beer product is fine for a Top 40 or Album-Oriented Rock (AOR) station, but an alternative, more suitable spot should be created for a Classic or Jazz radio station.

This chapter focuses on the high-risk-tool WHITE Cell goods and services. The following three chapters examine each of the remaining three product categories, namely the RED, BLUE, and YELLOW products. The chapters concentrate mainly on the substantive outcomes of the study and the meaning of the results. Only a brief explanation of the method of analysis used to evaluate the data is included. Interested readers who wish to know more about the technical details should refer to Appendix C and D.

Method of Analysis

To examine the performance of each creative element, the study used a two-group discriminant analysis. Though this statistical technique is quite sophisticated, its goal here is very simple: to classify a radio commercial as good (successful) or poor (unsuccessful) based solely on its creative features. To accomplish this, a mathematical model was developed that includes each of the creative elements that fall within the general creative categories of message style, structure, and presenter characteristics. The procedure identifies the strength and type of impact (positive/negative) that each element has on a commercial's performance. This type of analysis reveals patterns in the data and uncovers those characteristics regularly associated with good and poor radio commercials. Hence, given a commercial's creative make-up, it is possible to accurately predict how well it will perform.

To analyze the discriminating ability of each creative element, the selection of radio commercials was split into the four Product Color Matrix (PCM) categories. This led to sixteen separate discriminant models: one for each of the four dependent measures (i.e., communication index, proven recall, execution recall, and persuasion) in each of the four product cells. The results of this procedure will show which elements influenced the advertisement's performance and whether it had a positive or negative impact. To ensure that a clear distinction between the commercials was possible, the top 37% of the commercials were identified as good commercials and the bottom 37% were categorized as poor commercials. The middle 26% were classified as mediocre performers and were eliminated from the analysis. This approach is consistent with the belief that important relationships are most likely to be discovered by focusing on extreme levels of performance.

Predictive Performance

One method of evaluating the predictive ability of a discriminant model is to develop the model on one subset of the data and then test this solution on another subset of the data. For this data analysis, 60% of the commercials were used to develop the discriminant models, which were then tested for accuracy on the remaining 40%.

The predictive performance for each of the four discriminant models within each product category is presented in Figure 5–1.

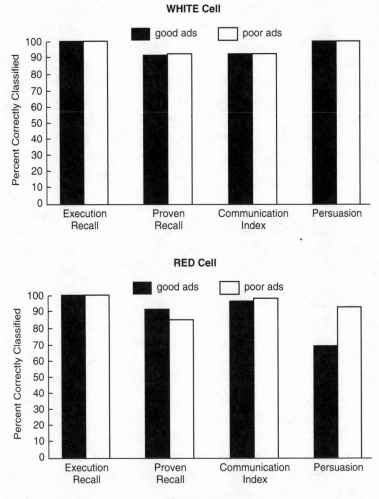

Figure 5–1

Predictive Performance for the Four Discriminant Models Within Each Product Category

Overall, the models did extremely well in predicting the performance of a commercial, and were particularly accurate in predicting the performance for WHITE Cell products. The accuracy of prediction ranged from 90.3% to 100% for good commercials and from 91.7% to 100% for poor commercials

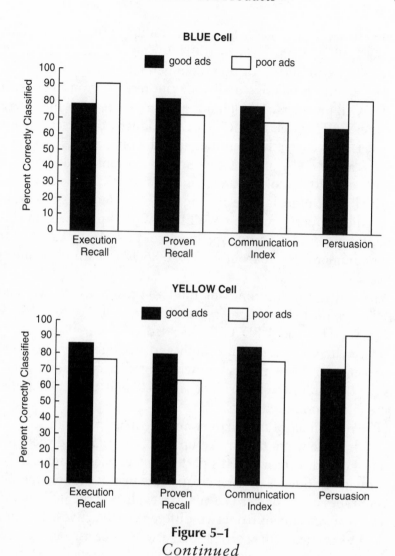

Figure 5–1
Continued

(see also Appendix D). These results provide assurance that the message style, message structure, and presenter factors are extremely good predictors of a commercial's performance for this set of products.

The predictive results for RED Cell commercials were also

quite strong. In this case, the predictability of the discriminant models ranged from 70% to 100% for good commercials and from 86.7% to 100% for poor commercials.

The strong predictive ability of the models continues with BLUE Cell products. Though not quite as accurate as they were for the WHITE Cell and RED Cell products, the discriminant models still correctly identified good commercials between 63.9% and 81.4% of the time and poor commercials between 67.5% and 90.6% of the time.

Finally, the models were also significant, though less accurate in predicting performance for YELLOW Cell products. In this case, the models' accuracy spanned from 64.3% to 92.9% for poor commercials and from 72.7% to 86.1% for good commercials.

Generally, the discriminant models proved to be accurate predictors of a commercial's performance. The two high-risk cells (WHITE and RED Cells) yielded excellent discriminant models with an extraordinary ability to separate poor and good commercials. While not as overwhelmingly accurate, the models developed for the low-risk cells (BLUE and YELLOW Cells) were fairly good predictors.

The remainder of this chapter and the next three examine the individual elements that make up a commercial and their impact on a radio commercial's performance. Each chapter looks at how the influence of each creative element varies for the different types of products. The analysis evaluated the influence of each creative element from two different perspectives. The first aspect examined is the correlation between a particular element and the discriminant function. This statistic shows the relationship between the element and the commercial's ability to enhance the communication index, proven and execution recall and persuasion. The tables used to portray this relationship (e.g., Table 5–1) include only those elements that had either a significant positive (+) or negative (–) association. The significance of the correlation is denoted by the number of pluses or minuses listed for each element. The higher the significance, the more likely that the element influenced the results. Thus, an el-

Table 5–1
*Correlation Between Message Style Elements
and Discriminant Function—WHITE Cell Products*

Style Element	Index	Proven	Execution	Persuasion
No Music	+++	+++	+++	+++
No Humor	+	+++	+++	+
Functional Mnemonics	+	+++	−	+++
Other Music	−−−	−−−	−−−	−−−

+++, −−−, $p \leq .05$.
+, −, $p > .05$.

ement with three plus signs would have a highly significant positive correlation with the discriminant function and would tend to lead to good performance.

The analysis continues by illustrating the presence of the elements in good and poor commercials. These tables (e.g., Tables 5–2) illustrate how often a good and poor commercial contains a particular element. For example, a 59.7% for Related Audio in good commercials indicates that 59.7% of the good commercials contained this particular element. To observe the overall creative structure of both good and poor commercials, these tables include all the creative elements, not just those that were statistically significant. This makes it possible to determine the creative profiles associated with both good and poor commercials. (Note: This analysis uses only the Proven Recall measure.)

The results of the analyses reveal some similarities across the product categories. However, there are also some important variations that give a unique profile of those features that contribute to the success of a radio commercial. When consistent relationships can be uncovered, advertisers will be able to use a radio's creative composition to predict its eventual performance.

What Works for WHITE Cell Products

To reiterate, WHITE Cell products are high-risk, functional items, such as appliances, business goods and services, insur-

Table 5–2

*Presence of Message Style Elements in Good
and Poor Radio Commercials—WHITE Cell
Products (Proven Recall Only)*

Style Element	Overall (%) (all commercials)	Good (%) (top 37% only)	Poor (%) (bottom 37% only)
Humor			
No Humor	86.9*	96.1	79.7
Related Humor	7.7	1.6	13.2
Unrelated Humor	6.4	3.3	7.1
	100.0	100.0	100.0
Music			
No Music	48.3*	77.4	27.4
Jingles	7.3	9.7	2.4
Singing Music	4.3	0.0	6.0
Other Music	40.1	12.9	64.2
	100.0	100.0	100.0
Audio			
Related Audio	68.8	59.7	71.4
Unrelated Audio	31.2	40.3	28.6
	100.0	100.0	100.0
Commercial Origin			
TV Sound	0.0	0.0	0.0
TV Version	6.3	0.0	1.2
Radio Sound	93.7	100.0	98.8
	100.0	100.0	100.0
Mnemonics			
No Mnemonics	39.7	33.9	52.4
Functional	58.4*	66.1	46.4
Non-Functional	1.9	0.0	1.2
Fantasy	0.0	0.0	0.0
	100.0	100.0	100.0
Something New	16.1	9.7	20.2

*Denotes significant difference between good and poor commercials.

ance, and banking products and services. Consumers will spend a considerable amount of time and thought when considering the purchase of these items. Prospective buyers will be motivated to pay more attention to message content and the primary selling points of the message and less to unrelated message features. Hence, informational cues pertaining to the attributes of these "Tools" should be more successful than peripheral cues.

Structurally, commercials in the WHITE Cell:

- rarely use humor
- tend not to use music
- show the heaviest use of functional mnemonics
- have the lowest use of something new
- mostly use the announcer format, although it is used less here than in the other cells
- have the highest use of the Testimonial, Interview, and Problem Solution formats
- show the highest use of sixty-second length
- include the most words
- have the highest amount of brand mentions
- include the most number of ideas
- have the highest use of male-only presenters

Message Style Elements—WHITE Cell Products

It is clear that within the set of message style elements, good commercials tend not to contain humor or music, but do include functional mnemonics. As can be seen in Table 5–1, these elements have a strong positive correlation with a commercial's performance. Note that the more peripheral element of "Other Music" (i.e., background music) has a negative influence on a commercial's performance.

A broader and more complete picture comes into view when the presence of each style element is examined for good and poor commercials (Table 5–2). This analysis shows that 77.4% of the good commercials contained no music, while only 27% of the poor ads did not use music. A large number (64.3%) of poor commercials used Other Music. This leads to the obvious conclusion that, in this category, music is not associated with good advertising and "other music" especially leads to poor performance for WHITE Cell products. This information provides a strong signal that advertisers should be very cautious about using music for WHITE Cell products. These products may be deemed as being more serious types of products; hence creative elements that may be considered to be superficial and less serious would not have a positive influence.

Another factor that comes to light is the use of humor and mnemonics in WHITE Cell commercials. The absence of humor is much more prevalent in good commercials (96.1%) than poor commercials (79.7%). In fact, Related and Unrelated Humor are rarely (1.6% and 3.2%, respectively) found in good commercials in this product category. Conversely, the use of functional mnemonics appears to have an advantageous effect. Good commercials were more likely (66.1%) to use a mnemonic device than those which did not incorporate a mnemonics device (33.9%).

Finally, the prospect of including "Something New" in the message did not lead to good commercial performance. A significant number (20%) of poor commercials touted some new idea or concept, while only a relatively few (9.7%) good commercials mentioned something new. New ideas do not seem to go over well for WHITE Cell products.

Success with Serious Radio

Utilizing the important elements characteristically found in effective commercials in the WHITE Cell (i.e., no humor or music, and not introducing a new idea or product), RisCassi & Davis law firm, a Hartford, Connecticut–based firm that has specialized in personal injury cases since the 1940s, has had great success with serious radio.

Although the law firm had never relied on advertising to promote its services, when other firms in the area began to heavily run television commercials RisCassi & Davis felt that they, too, needed to develop a comprehensive communications strategy. With the help of Gold & Ward, a marketing strategy firm based in Avon, Connecticut, RisCassi & Davis decided to advertise and chose radio as its only communications medium. According to Gold & Ward's president, Peter Gold, "With radio, RisCassi & Davis could virtually own the airwaves because few other firms utilize the medium."

Gold sought the creative assistance of Joy Golden, president of New York City–based Joy Radio, to create a straightforward, serious commercial (voiced by one man) without music for the law firm to reach its target demographic of adults aged twenty-five to sixty-four. Over an eighteen-month period, three sixty-second spots ran four weeks on, eight weeks off. "Our objective was to start in strong over a four-week period, take a brief hiatus, and then reinforce our message again for another four weeks," said Gold. The spots ran during morning and afternoon drive times on approximately five AM and FM stations (including News/Talk, Adult Contemporary, and Soft Rock) in the Hartford/New Haven area.

"Actual figures are proprietary," according to Gold, "but RisCassi & Davis has seen a *significant increase* in the number of cases they have taken on as a direct result of its radio advertising."[1,2] [COMMERCIAL 3 ON DISC]

Message Structure Elements—WHITE Cell Products

Eight of the message structure elements had a positive relationship and two had a negative association with a commercial's performance (Table 5–3). The most consistent variables included: the number of words in the commercial, the number of times the brand was mentioned, and the length of the commercial. Hence, the more words in a commercial and the more often the brand is identified, the higher the likelihood that the commercial for WHITE Cell products will perform well.

The positive impact of the length of the commercials is further illustrated in Table 5–4, where most (90.3%) of the good commercials were sixty seconds long. Conversely, only 26.2%

Table 5–3

Correlation Between Message Structure Elements and Discriminant Function—WHITE Cell Products

Structure Element	Index	Proven	Execution	Persuasion
Number of Words	+++	+++	+++	+++
Number of Mentions	+++	+++	+++	+++
60" Length	+++	+++	+++	+++
Testimonial Format	+++	+++	+++	–
Number of Ideas	+++	+++	+++	–––
Problem Format	+++	+++	–––	+++
Interview Format	+++	+++	+++	–
Number of Message Reps	+	+++	+++	–
Announcer Format	–––	–––	–––	–––
Slice of Life Format	–––	–––	–––	–

+++, –––, $p \leq .05$.
+, –, $p > .05$.

of the poor commercials were sixty seconds in length. Radio commercials for WHITE Cell products perform better when they are longer and contain more information. This may be due to the importance of the product being advertised and the willingness of the audience to concentrate on message content. These results were consistent across all four response categories, further indicating the importance of including as many brand mentions and pertinent ideas as possible in the commercial.

Of particular importance to the structuring of a radio commercial is the decision of which creative format will work best. On the negative side, commercials that used Announcer and Slice of Life formats, had a negative correlation with the four response categories (Table 5–3). This indicates that these formats led to a less than optimal performance. However, when looking at the structure of good and poor commercials it is clear that the Testimonial, Interview, and Problem Solution formats lead to more successful commercials (Table 5–4). These formats were much more prevalent in good as opposed to poor commercials.

To summarize, on the average, good commercials for WHITE Cell products had more words and more mentions of

Table 5–4
*Presence of Message Structure Elements in Good
and Poor Radio Commercials—WHITE Cell Products
(Proven Recall Only)*

Structure Element	Overall (all commercials)	Good (top 37% only)	Poor (bottom 37% only)
Format			
Testimonial	17.0%*	36.5%	4.8%
Interview	13.9%*	19.3%	4.8%
Slice of Life	16.5%*	3.2%	26.0%
Problem Solution	12.0%*	22.6%	2.4%
Demonstration	0.0%	0.0%	0.0%
Announcer	41.6%*	19.4%	63.0%
	100.0%	100.0%	100.0%
Mechanical			
60" Length	60.3%*	77.4%	27.4%
Number of Words	134*	168	101
Entry Time	9	8.2	9.4
No. of Brand Mentions	6*	7.7	4.1
Number of Ideas	6*	7.0	6.3
No. of Message Reps	3*	3.4	2.8

*Denotes significant difference between good and poor commercials.

the brand name. The Slice of Life and Announcer formats did not contribute to performance as 26% of the poor commercials included the former and a huge 63.1% the latter. Clearly, the use of the Announcer format is not advisable in the WHITE Cell to the large extent that it has been used in the past.

Selling with Repetition and Consistency

The W. S. Palmer Company, an independent insurance broker with locations in Tulare, Exeter, and Sacramento, California, utilized an important element of the WHITE Cell—namely repetition—to expand its business and increase its name awareness within the local communities. Traditionally, the broker ran advertisements in local newspapers and direct mailers to attempt to reach its target of middle- to upper-income homeowners aged twenty-five to fifty-four, but never experienced an increase in office traffic.

W. S. Palmer turned to radio because of its ability to generate immediate responses from listeners by frequently mentioning its name and phone number during the course of a sixty-second spot. Listeners were asked to phone W. S. Palmer to receive a competitive quote on homeowner's insurance—right over the phone. The spots, voiced by a male radio personality, ran for nine consecutive months on one radio station—Adult Contemporary-formatted KSEQ FM, based in Tulare/Visalia, California.

According to Greg Todd, a W. S. Palmer representative, "Immediately after our first radio ad ran on March 1st [1993] we received 25 callers asking for a quote. And, we continued to receive calls even four days after the initial spot stopped airing."

The reason for the swift success? The straightforward W. S. Palmer radio spots consisted of basic, no-nonsense, informative elements—company name and locations, and the repetition of the various phone numbers where listeners could call for a fast, over-the-phone quote on homeowner's insurance.[3]

Selling with Testimonials

Experiencing equal success with radio is the Lo Jack Stolen Vehicle Recovery System—a device that electronically tips off police to the location of stolen cars. Using radio testimonials and "demonstrations," Lo Jack exceeded sales projections during its 1990 launch in Los Angeles. Lo Jack was initially sold through an 800-number telemarketing program as well as through 100 new car dealers that sold the product as an accessory. "With the 1990 launch in Los Angeles, we ran one fractional space ad in the *Los Angeles Times,* but we knew that radio would be our main advertising medium because so many people live in their cars here," said Kathleen Krogius, Vice President/Account Supervisor for Sacks/Fuller, Lo Jack's agency-of-record. "Radio is the most effective way to reach customers when they are behind the wheels of their cars."

To create excitement about the product, Lo Jack ran spots on eight Southern California radio stations for three weeks before the units became available. Following the launch, Lo Jack utilized a total of fifteen stations each quarter, with five different stations running schedules every three weeks. Creatively, Lo Jack used live, sixty-second copy delivered by morning drive personalities to take advantage of radio's immediacy, combined with high-impact testimonials of satisfied customers relating their experiences in having their stolen vehicles recovered, thanks to Lo Jack. Additionally, several morning radio personalities tested the product on the air, using their assistants as drivers of a Lo Jack–equipped stolen car. All vehicles were tracked within a matter of minutes.

According to the Director of Marketing and Sales at Lo Jack, John W. Raber, in addition to far exceeding sales goals after the initial 1990 radio launch, Lo Jack has significantly increased its radio advertising budget since 1990 as radio continues to yield solid results, and sales continue to rise. In fact, radio is the only medium Lo Jack utilizes.[4,5] [COMMERCIAL 4 ON DISC]

Presenter Characteristics—WHITE Cell Products

The final category of creative factors includes the characteristics of the presenters used in the commercial. Some interesting results are found within this creative category. Generally, the number of presenters and the use of both men and women as presenters had a positive effect on performance (Table 5–5).

Table 5–5

Correlation Between Presenter Characteristics and Discriminant Function—WHITE Cell Products

Presenter Characteristic	Index	Proven	Execution	Persuasion
Number of Presenters	+++	+++	+++	+++
Both Male and Female	+	+++	+++	+

+++, ---, $p \leq .05$.
+, -, $p > .05$.

The number of presenters had a strong positive influence on three of the four response categories, whereas the use of men and women had a positive effect on all four of the response categories.

Table 5–6 shows that, on the average, good commercials for WHITE Cell products tended to use more presenters (2.6) than poor commercials (1.8). This table also illustrates that over 48% of the good commercials used both men and women while only 22.6% of the poor commercials included both sexes. It is notable that many (77.3%) of the poor commercials used only a male presenter. Interestingly, there is a total absence of women as the sole presenter for WHITE Cell products. This absence makes it impossible to determine how female-only presenters would perform for these types of products. Though the use of men as presenters predominates in this set of products, the results indicate that it is not generally associated with good commercials.

Table 5–6

*Presence of Presenter Characteristics in Good
and Poor Radio Commercials—WHITE Cell Products
(Proven Recall Only)*

Presenter Characteristic	Overall (all commercials)	Good (top 37% only)	Poor (bottom 37% only)
Gender			
Male	63.7%	51.6%	77.4%
Female	0.0%	0.0%	0.0%
Both Together	36.3%	48.4%	22.6%
	100.0%	100.0%	100.0%
Age			
Adult	97.8%	96.8%	100.0%
Teen	1.3%	3.2%	0.0%
Mixed Adult/Other	0.9%	0.0%	0.0%
	100.0%	100.0%	100.0%
Number of Presenters	3.0	2.6	1.8

*Denotes significant difference between good and poor commercials.

Promoting Serious Issues

Shortly after the 1992 riots that took place in Los Angeles, a local television station, KNBC TV, ran an investigative report entitled "Women and Guns and Why" that discussed the rapid increase in women purchasing guns to protect themselves. In addition to the television station's own on-air spots promoting the report, they sought the help of radio to reach women who may not have been regular viewers of their station.

Chuck Blore, CEO of The Chuck Blore Company, wrote a spot—"I Bought a Gun"—targeted to women over twenty-five who were married and had children. The commercial had all the important elements of a successful WHITE Cell spot: namely a male and female presenter, no background music, and no humor. The spot opens with the husband coming home from work and asking, "How was your day?" only to hear his wife respond "I bought a gun . . . I bought a gun. And I'll use it if I have to . . . ". The spot ran during the week of the report and generated more inquiries at KNBC than any other spot promoting their special reports.

"Audiences have come to trust radio," said Blore. "So when there is a feeling within a radio spot that an audience can relate to, or when that feeling is already inside the listener, radio works. The "I Bought a Gun" spot was so successful for KNBC because it really hit home for many, many radio listeners."[6] [COMMERCIAL 5 ON DISC]

A Summary of What Works in the WHITE Cell

The analysis at the beginning of the chapter provides some evidence that, within reason, the performance of a commercial can be predetermined by knowing its creative make-up. Hence, the communication ability and the persuasiveness of the commercial may be evaluated by analyzing its creative make-up (i.e., message style, structure, and presenter characteristics).

In general, an interesting pattern emerges for this set of commercials, yielding a profile of what does and doesn't work for radio commercials promoting WHITE Cell products. As might be expected for these high-risk tools, elements that focused on message information increased the performance of the commercials. Conversely, those elements that can be identified as peripheral cues had little or negative impact.

Commercials that avoided the use of music and humor performed better than commercials that used these elements. The serious nature of the products in this cell probably does not blend well with creative elements that are too "light-hearted." Generally, commercials performed rather poorly when humor and/or music was used.

Commercial formats that tend to be more serious in nature performed well in this cell. The Testimonial, Interview, and Problem Solution format worked well for WHITE Cell products. This is consistent with the tool aspect of these products where audience members would be receptive to functional information. Conversely, the Slice of Life and Announcer formats may provide little functional value nor reduce risk. This may be particularly true if the announcer is not deemed to be a credible source. Also consistent with the need to reduce risk is the indication that longer and more informative commercials worked well in this cell. Longer commercials in terms of length, words, additional ideas, and brand mentions all contributed to good performance.

The findings suggest that commercials that used humor and music should be avoided in favor of other approaches. Other, more thought-provoking tactics (e.g., functional mnemonics) may work best for commercials in this product category. Less consistent with the findings is the relatively heavy use of the Announcer format, men as presenters, and thirty-second commercials. The extensive use of these factors is puzzling in light of their high association with poor commercial performance. The question arises as to why these elements are used so often when they are so strongly associated with poor commercials. One interesting finding was the association of "Something New" with the poor commercials. Given that additional information appears to be welcomed for commercials in this cell, it is surpris-

	Worked Well	Did Not Work Well
All Response Measures	No humor No music 60" length More words More brand mentions	Other music Slice of life format Announcer format
Proven Recall	Functional mnemonics Testimonial format Interview format Problem solution format More ideas More message repetitions More presenters	Humor Something new

Figure 5–2

What Works and Doesn't Work in the WHITE Cell

ing that this element had a negative influence. It may be that the audience is looking for information to solve certain purchase decisions and not willing to process information pertaining to new issues.

Chapter 6

Anatomy of a Good Commercial for High-Risk Toys—RED Cell Products

A blind pig may sometimes find truffles, but it helps if he foreages in an oak forest.

—David Ogilvy and Joel Raphaelson 1982

What Works for RED Cell Products

I tems in the RED Cell include products and services that are considered to be of higher risk and more experiential. These include the toys for which consumers will not only devote more attention to their commercials but will also be likely to have an emotional connection with the product. Products in the RED Cell include items such as hair coloring, grooming aids, fashion clothing, and sports cars. The increased risk factors associated with the product should lead consumers to pay more attention to message content and informational cues. However, the experiential aspects associated with the toys should make the audience more susceptible to emotional creative elements.

Structurally, commercials in the RED Cell:

- show the lowest use of humor
- usually include some type of music
- are heaviest users of jingles

- have the highest use of related audio
- use only radio sound origin
- show that about half use functional mnemonics
- are the heaviest users of the Announcer format
- tend to be evenly split between thirty-second and sixty-second length
- are the next to lowest in the number of words in the commercial
- use a male only presenter in about half the commercials
- are the highest users of female-only presenters

Message Style Elements—RED Cell Products

Three message style elements had a positive effect on commercial performance for RED products and four had a negative effect. Those commercials that did not use music or any mnemonics tended to perform better than those that did include these elements. Also, commercials that used related humor tended to perform well. Elements that led to poor commercial performance included the use of both functional and non-functional mnemonics, singing music, and the absence of humor.

Table 6–2 highlights each style element and identifies those that are related to good and poor commercial performance for RED Cell products. This table shows that related humor is

Table 6–1

Correlation Between Message Style Elements and Discriminant Function—RED Cell Products

Style Element	Index	Proven	Execution	Persuasion
No music	+++	+++	+++	0
No Mnemonics	+++	+	+++	−
Related Humor	+	+++	+	−
Singing Music	−−−	−−−	−−−	−
Non-functional Mnemonics	−−−	−	−−−	0
Functional Mnemonics	−−−	−	−	−
No Humor	−	−−−	−	+

+++, −−−, $p \leq .05$.
+, −, $p > .05$.

Table 6–2
*Presence of Message Style Elements
in Good and Poor Radio Commercials—
RED Cell Products (Proven Recall Only)*

Style Element	Overall (%) (all commercials)	Good (%) (top 37% only)	Poor (%) (bottom 37% only)
Humor			
No Humor	89.0*	77.8	96.3
Related Humor	8.9*	20.0	3.7
Unrelated Humor	2.1	2.2	0.0
	100.0*	100.0	100.0
Music			
No Music	16.1	28.9	3.7
Jingles	43.2	24.4	37.0
Singing Music	16.7	8.9	37.1
Other Music	24.0	37.8	22.2
	100.0	100.0	100.0
Audio			
Related Audio	83.9	73.3	77.8
Unrelated Audio	16.1	26.7	22.2
	100.0	100.0	100.0
Commercial Origin			
TV Sound	0.0	0.0	0.0
TV Version	0.0	0.0	0.0
Radio Sound	100.0	100.0	100.0
	100.0	100.0	100.0
Mnemonics			
No Mnemonics	46.4*	48.9	37.0
Functional	50.5*	51.1	59.3
Non-functional	3.1	0.0	3.7
Fantasy	0.0	0.0	0.0
	100.0	100.0	100.0
Something New	16.1	16.6	14.8

*Denotes significant difference between good and poor commercials.

found five times more often (20.0%) in good rather than poor commercials (3.7%). Also, the absence of music was found seven times more often (28.9%) in good commercials as opposed to poor commercials (3.7%). Other, or background, music had a favorable effect as it was found in 37.8% of the good commercials compared to being in only 22.2% of the poor advertisements.

Singing music seemed to have an adverse effect on commercial performance. This element was found four times as often (37.0%) in poor as in good commercials (8.9%). Jingles also appeared to be somewhat harmful to commercial performance as 38% of the poor commercials contained some type of jingle while only 24.4% of the good commercials used this element.

The use of mnemonics in the radio commercials produced some interesting results. Commercials that did not use a mnemonic device performed much better than those that did use some type of mnemonic device.

Selling Boots with Related Humor

Even though related humor was found in only 20% of the good ads, the results indicate that it can effectively contribute to good performance for RED Cell products. If a spot is created properly and creatively, related humor can be an effective selling approach. For example, Thieves Market, a chain of boot stores in the Los Angeles area, has utilized humorous radio relating to its products and outdoor advertising since 1990 to build its image and raise awareness as *the* place to buy boots. "The large, Los Angeles radio market offers an effective, cost-efficient way to reach the chain's primary target of adults twenty-five to thirty-four," said Cary Sacks, Partner and Creative Director of Sacks/Fuller Advertising, Thieves Market's advertising-agency-of-record.

The radio campaign uses image- and awareness-building spots throughout the year, interspersed with humorous sale spots during key periods to drive customers immediately in the door. Some of the dozens of radio spots over the years have featured such themes as conversations between the various pairs of "mundane" shoes found in the average closet and how each particular shoe reacts when the newcomer—a hip pair of boots purchased at Thieves Market—joins the bottom-of-the-closet denizens and a parody of "The Little Boy who Cried Wolf" tell-ing the story of how other boot stores cry "Sale, Sale!" all the time without really meaning it, while Thieves Market has only two huge sales per year.

The advertising campaign has not only expanded awareness, but has also enabled Thieves Market to more than double its stores in two years and post three consecutive years of double-digit per-store sales increases. According to Sacks, the reason for the success is simple. "Radio is the freest medium of them all," commented Sacks. "You're not restricted by what you see. You can create your own world."[1,2] [COMMERCIALS 6–9 ON DISC]

Message Structure Elements—RED Cell Products

Only two message structure elements were consistently related to commercial performance. The number of words included in the commercial and sixty-second commercials increased the communication index, proven and execution recall of the commercial (Table 6–3). Not surprisingly, the longer commercials led to a better understanding and higher recall for RED Cell product commercials. Since these are high-risk products, the audience will be willing and motivated to devote more attention to the commercial. Interestingly, these factors had little effect on the persuasion factor. Hence, the length of the commercial will help audience recall, but other creative elements need to be integrated into the message in order to achieve maximum selling impact.

Table 6–3

Correlation Between Message Structure Elements and Discriminant Function—RED Cell Products

Structure Element	Index	Proven	Execution	Persuasion
Number of Words	+++	+++	+++	–
Number of Mentions	+++	+++	+++	–

+++, ---, $p \leq .05$.
+, –, $p > .05$.

The lack of any other significant structure elements is in sharp contrast to the results found in the other high-risk category (i.e., WHITE Cell), where several commercial formats influenced performance. However, some insight is gained with a deeper look at Table 6–4. Though not statistically significant, there is an indication that some commercial formats may work well for products in the RED Cell. These formats, which include Testimonials, Interview, Problem Solution, and Demonstration, were more frequently associated with good rather than poor commercials. Again, the Announcer format led to less favorable results.

Table 6–4

Presence of Message Structure Elements in Good and Poor Radio Commercials— RED Cell Products (Proven Recall Only)

Structure Element	Overall (all commercials)	Good (top 37% only	Poor (bottom 37% only)
Format			
Testimonial	2.6%	4.0%	0.0%
Interview	1.6%	2.0%	0.0%
Slice of Life	2.6%	4.0%	4.0%
Problem Solution	7.2%	11.0%	4.0%
Demonstration	2.1%	7.0%	0.0%
Announcer	83.9%	71.0%	93.0%
	100.0%	100.0%	100.0%
Mechanical			
60" Length	52.6%*	66.7%	29.6%
Number of Words	101*	118	86
Entry Time	8	8.6	9
No. of Brand Mentions	6	6.8	6.7
Number of Ideas	4	4.6	3.9
No. of Message Reps	3	3.1	3.2

*Denotes significant difference between good and poor commercials.

Testimonials to Life Reach Women, Sell Fashionable Shoes

L. A. Gear, a Los Angeles–based manufacturer of casual fashion footwear, uses radio to increase awareness of its "hip and exciting" line of shoes. The sixty-second spots, utilizing important RED Cell characteristics, are read by one woman with an opening and closing male voiceover, and they contain, on the average, more than 185 words.

The reason for radio? In-house research had shown that radio—particularly radio in the summer months—would effectively reach L. A. Gear's target of women aged eighteen to thirty-four. According to L. A. Gear's Director of Creative Services, Adam Bleibtrau, "We chose to use very visual images on radio in a creative manner. This 1991 campaign was our first time on radio and we used it as our primary summer advertising, with some support from print." L. A. Gear ran two- to three-week flights during morning and afternoon drive times throughout the summer in the top ten markets across the United States, and according to Bleibtrau, "The results were beyond our expectations."

Not only did the sales results indicate that the campaign was extremely effective in increasing brand awareness, but the publicity generated by the spots was enormous. "Many radio stations did take-offs and spoofs of the commercials. Several national magazines, including *Playboy,* wrote about us. And, we sent out over 300 copies of the script to radio listeners who phoned us," explained Bleibtrau.[3,4] [COMMERCIALS 10–11 ON DISC]

SCRIPT: L. A. GEAR/FANTASIES OF A SINGLE GIRL

With more than 185 words in a sixty-second spot, the L. A. Gear "Single Girl" series reflects what Message Structure Elements work well in the RED Cell category. Below is a script from one of the three spots created for this campaign. All spots were written by Jennifer Joseph, a San Diego–based freelance writer.

VOICEOVER: Fantasies of a Single Girl . . . Brought to you by L. A. Gear.

FEMALE VOICE: Before he loves you for ever and ever 'til death do you part, and showers you with red roses and candy, and does your laundry, and cooks you dinner, and asks you what commitment means to you, and carries your picture around in his wallet at all times, and answers the questions to the "Hot Lover's Test" in this month's *Cosmo* with you, and buys you a big diamond ring and earrings to match, and carries your books, and goes antiquing with your dad, and feeds your cats tuna, and puts up with your mother, and is willing to watch mushy love stories with you on your VCR, and goes with you to the local salad bar instead of ordering pizza, and makes your bed, and listens to your funky music instead of pure rock and roll, and brags to his friends how smart you are, and loves your body exactly the way it is, and tolerates your big flannel nightie with the little yellow ducks on it, and becomes the father of your children, he has to call back.

VOICEOVER: L. A. Gear . . . have a nice day.

Presenter Characteristics—RED Cell Products

Similar to the message style and message structure elements, the presenter category in the RED Cell was quite distinct from that in the WHITE Cell. You will recall that in the WHITE Cell additional presenters and the combined use of men and women had a positive effect on commercial performance (Table 6–5).

Table 6–5

Correlation Between Presenter Characteristics and Discriminant Function—RED Cell Products

Presenter Characteristic	Index	Proven	Execution	Persuasion
Male	+++	+	+++	+
Number of Presenters	---	-	---	-

+++, ---, $p \leq .05$.
+, -, $p > .05$.

However, in the RED Cell, the number of presenters had a negative impact, with more presenters leading to poor performance. Only the use of male presenters seemed to improve commercial performance (Table 6–6). Interestingly, in this product category female-only presenters appeared in poor commercials almost four times more often (26.9%) than in good commercials (6.7%).

Demonstrating Car Stereos with Radio

Alpine Car Stereos of Toronto, Canada utilized many of the important elements found in the RED Cell: a male speaker was the only voice present while a demonstration of the product—through music—brought to life the richness of the product.

Alpine Car Stereos has utilized radio since it began selling products many years ago: "With the nature of our product, radio is a natural given," said a company spokesperson. To

Table 6–6
Presence of Presenter Characteristics
in Good and Poor Radio Commercials—
RED Cell Products (Proven Recall Only)

Presenter Characteristic	Overall (all commercials)	Good (top 37% only)	Poor (bottom 37% only)
Gender			
Male	50.8%*	60.0%	48.0%
Female	18.8%	6.7%	26.0%
Both Together	30.4%	33.3%	26.0%
	100.0%	100.0%	100.0%
Age			
Adult	98.4%	97.8%	100.0%
Teen	1.6%	2.2%	0.0%
Mixed Adult/Other	0.0%	0.0%	0.0%
	100.0%	100.0%	100.0%
Number of Presenters	2.0*	2.0	2.4

*Denotes significant difference between good and poor commercials.

reach its primary and secondary targets of men aged eighteen to nineteen and thirty to fifty-five, respectively, Alpine sought the creative assistance of Toronto-based Harris, Cole, Wilde Productions, Inc., a radio and television production company. The most recent radio campaign consisted of two, sixty-second spots that ran on Rock and All Sports radio stations in major markets throughout Canada, including Toronto, Montreal, Vancouver, Calgary, and Edmonton. Both spots consist of a guitar music bed in the background, while a laid-back male voice describes the career of a talented, yet unlikely, blues musician named Eric Clapton, and about the hidden guitar player who is transformed when the spotlight hits him. The tagline follows: "Serious music that deserves serious car audio. Alpine . . . very simply the best car CD players and audio systems you can buy."

"Alpine Car Stereos is in a leading position in the marketplace and we believe that radio has played a very important role in the promotion of our brand name," concluded the company spokesperson.[5] [COMMERCIAL 12 ON DISC]

A Summary of What Works in the RED Cell

Though the products and services in the RED Cell have a similar risk factor as those in the WHITE Cell, the experiential aspects associated with these "toys" make them quite distinct from the "Tools." Some executional devices have a common impact on the two product categories, but some emotional cues seem to play a more important role for RED Cell products. Devices, such as humor, seemed to work well in the RED Cell. Comparatively, these devices did not perform well for the more functional WHITE Cell. A summary of what works and doesn't work for RED Cell products is illustrated in Figure 6–1.

Although music is commonly used for commercials in this cell, it seems to have a negative influence on performance. This was especially true for singing music and jingles, which were significantly related to poor performance.

Commercials that used related humor tended to outperform those that did not include humor. The experiential aspect asso-

	Worked Well	Did Not Work Well
All Response Measures	No music Male presenters	Singing music Functional mnemonics Non-functional mnemonics More presenters
Proven Recall	Related humor No mnemonics 60" length More words More ideas Problem solution format Testimonial format Interview format Demonstration format More ideas Male/female presenter together	No humor Jingles Announcer format Female presenter

Figure 6–1

What Works and Doesn't Work in the RED Cell

ciated with these "toys," added to the relative risk factor, suggests humor can be effective as long as it relates to the message.

Unlike its impact in the WHITE Cell, functional mnemonics had a negative impact on commercials for RED Cell products. In fact, those commercials that did not include any type of mnemonic performed better than those that did use a mnemonic device. Not surprisingly, longer commercials led to better performance. As was the case with the WHITE Cell commercials, the increased risk associated with these products indicates that the audience will be more willing to accept and process additional information.

As with the WHITE Cell commercials, the Announcer format had a negative impact on performance. However, once again it was the most commonly used format, leading to the continuing question of "Why are these elements being used so much if they are not working?"

The results presented in this chapter (and the previous chapter) indicate that risk factors related to both the WHITE and RED Cells lead some creative elements to have a similar influence on their respective commercials. However, the "toy" aspect associated with the RED Cell led to another set of creative elements that has a very different effect in this cell than it did in the WHITE Cell.

Chapter 7

Anatomy of a Good Commercial for Low-Risk Tools—BLUE Cell Products

Sit down before facts as a little child, be prepared to give up every preconceived notion, follow humbly wherever and to whatever abyss nature leads, or you shall learn nothing.

—*T. H. Huxley*

This chapter investigates the components that lead to good and poor radio commercials for low-risk "little tools"— products that are purchased quite often and require less consumer attention on message content because the purchase is usually routine and given little thought. These products reside in the BLUE Cell and include such items as cleaning supplies, cooking accessories, and personal hygiene goods. Other examples include functional products such as gasoline products, toothpaste, and detergents.

Combined, the two low-risk categories (BLUE and YELLOW Cells) account for almost 75% of the sample of radio commercials. Hence this, and the next chapter, will be of particular importance to most radio advertisers. Given the low level of perceived risk associated with these products and the almost routine purchase of them, the creative elements that contribute to good commercial performance should be much different than those that were associated with the high-risk (WHITE and RED) products.

Structurally, commercials in the BLUE Cell:

- tend not to use humor, but to a greater extent than WHITE and RED Cells
- tend not to use music
- have the second highest combined use of functional and non-functional mnemonics
- mostly use the Announcer format
- are the heaviest users of thirty-second spots
- include the least amount of words
- have the fewest brand mentions
- tend to use male-only presenters

What Works for BLUE Cell Products

BLUE Cell products are characterized by their low-perceived-risk and functional aspects. Consumers approach the purchase of these products in a rational manner with little emotional or sensory input. Given the relatively low risk and routine behavior associated with the purchase of these products, the audience will be unwilling to pay a great deal of attention to the information contained in a radio commercial. Therefore, creative features that are factually oriented should not be particularly effective in the BLUE Cell. Formats that use a more informational approach, such as demonstrations, problem solution, or interview techniques, should lead to below-average commercial performance. On the other hand, tactics that are more peripherally related, such as music, humor, and presenter characteristics, should enhance commercial performance.

Message Style Elements—BLUE Cell Products

Three of the message style elements had a significant relationship with the discriminant models developed for the BLUE Cell commercials (Table 7–1). Mnemonics (both functional and non-functional) and related humor generally had a positive ef-

Table 7-1
Correlation Between Message Style Elements
and Discriminant Function—BLUE Cell Products

Style Element	Index	Proven	Execution	Persuasion
Functional Mnemonics	+	+++	+++	+
Non-functional Mnemonics	+++	+++	+	+
Related Humor	+++	+	+++	−
No Mnemonics	−−−	−−−	−	−
Something New	−−−	−	−−−	−
No Humor	−−−	−−−	−−−	+

+++, −−−, $p \leq .05$.
+, −, $p > .05$.

fect on performance. Three elements had a negative influence on performance. These included the absence of both mnemonics and humor and the use of "something new" in the messages. However, while the absence of humor had a negative effect on the communication index, proven and execution recall factors, it inexplicably had a slightly positive impact on persuasion.

A consistency with the correlation results is apparent when the presence of the various creative elements is examined for both good and poor commercials for BLUE Cell products. Over 45% of the good commercials for BLUE Cell products used a functional mnemonic, while only 31.4% of the poor commercials used this tactic. Additionally, almost 68% of the poor commercials in the BLUE Cell did not include a mnemonic device. Also, the use of humor appears to be a valuable tool for BLUE Cell commercials. Almost 31% of the good commercials used related humor, while over 64% of the poor commercials did not include any type of humor.

Related Humor Sells Potatoes

The Potato Marketing Board of Prince Edward Island (P.E.I.) in Canada began using radio in 1991 to create and maintain

Table 7-2

Presence of Message Style Elements
in Good and Poor Radio Commercials—
BLUE Cell Products (Proven Recall Only)

Style Element	Overall (%) (all commercials)	Good (%) (top 37% only)	Poor (%) (bottom 37% only)
Humor			
No Humor	64.4*	52.3	64.2
Related Humor	22.0	30.8	22.9
Unrelated	13.6	16.9	12.9
	100.0	100.0	100.0
Music			
No Music	40.5	35.8	44.0
Jingles	12.2	11.0	11.0
Singing Music	9.5	9.9	8.0
Other Music	37.8	34.9	37.0
	100.0	100.0	100.0
Audio			
Related Audio	72.2	66.3	70.7
Unrelated Audio	27.8	33.7	29.3
	100.0	100.0	100.0
Commercial Origin			
TV Sound	0.0	0.0	0.0
TV Version	3.5	0.0	3.6
Radio Sound	96.5	100.0	96.4
	100.0	100.0	100.0
Mnemonics			
No Mnemonics	58.2*	42.4	67.9
Functional	37.1*	45.3	31.1
Non-functional	4.7	9.3	0.0
Fantasy	0.0	2.9	1.0
	100.0	100.0	100.0
Something New	18.0	15.7	17.9

*Denotes significant difference between good and poor commercials.

awareness of their high-quality brand of potatoes, and to cost-effectively target a large number of people. To reach P.E.I. Potatoes' target of women aged thirty-five to fifty-five, the Board sought the help of Media Concepts, based on Charlotte-town, P.E.I., who wrote a series of humorous spots that were performed by a local, popular comedy troupe called CODCO. Four spots were produced—each one a parody of Maritime life-style and the foods, specifically potatoes, that are consumed—and one spot was completely improvised by CODCO.

Running in the winter of 1991 in Atlantic Canada, Montreal, and Toronto on a variety of formats during early- and mid-morning drive times, the campaign generated tremendous success and dramatically increased awareness of P.E.I. Potatoes—so much so that the campaign was eventually expanded to include Quebec and Ontario. The spots were so unique and "hit home" to so many of the local radio listeners that a grocery store outside Halifax elaborated on the campaign by posting signs written as messages to the characters in the ads. One on-air radio personality in Halifax, after having a number of listeners comment on the ads, opened the phone lines for more discussion, and P.E.I. Potatoes received nearly a full hour of free air time as listeners talked about the creative spots—and the potatoes![1] [COMMERCIAL 13 ON DISC]

Functional Mnemonics and Sound Effects Double Sales and Awareness for Cepacol/Cepastat

Cepacol and Cepastat throat lozenges are becoming standard items in medicine chests across America and radio can be credited with their popularity. Cepacol Lozenges, introduced in 1945 by Marion Merrell Dow, soothe sore throat pain, while Cepastat Lozenges, introduced in 1976, help treat more serious sore throats. Aside from limited television advertising and physician sampling, neither brand had been significantly promoted until 1991 when all advertising dollars were placed into network and spot radio to promote both lozenges during the cough and cold season.

A series of creative radio commercials were produced—initially by Chiat Day and then by McElliott, Wright, Morrisson, & White—using sound effects to highlight the differences between sore throats and the medications used to treat them. The tagline explained the sound effects: "Cepacol for sore throats, and Cepastat for really, really sore throats."

According to the Brand Director for the two products, Dave Cook, "We easily exceeded our sales plan. With Cepacol we were 25% higher than expected and with Cepastat we surpassed our goal by 50%. Cepastat went from a relatively unknown product to number three on the market and experienced a 20% compounded growth from 1991 to 1994, further exemplifying the value of using consistent radio. When you utilize only one advertising vehicle and have a focused, tactical plan you can be sure that your advertising efforts have a direct relationship with your sale and market share increases."[2,3]

Message Structure Elements—BLUE Cell Products

Three message structure elements had a positive impact on the commercial performance in the BLUE Cell (Table 7–3). These included the number of times the brand was mentioned, the number of words in the message, and the length of the commercial. The more often the brand was mentioned, the more words

Table 7–3

Correlation Between Message Structure Elements and Discriminant Function—BLUE Cell Products

Structure Element	Index	Proven	Execution	Persuasion
Number of Mentions	+	+++	+++	+
Number of Words	+++	+++	+++	---
60" Length	+++	+++	+++	---
Number of Ideas	---	---	---	-
Announcer Format	---	---	---	-

+++, ---, $p \leq .05$.
+, -, $p > .05$.

in the commercial, and sixty-second commercials were all linked with good performance on the recall, communication, and comprehension measures. The effects of these features on the persuasion factor were somewhat mixed.

By contrast, two message structure elements had a negative effect on performance. The number of ideas in the message and the Announcer format led to poor performance. Thus, the more ideas a commercial contained, the poorer its performance. It seems that the audience will not devote much effort or attention to commercials for products that are routine purchases.

A broader view of the message structure elements that work for BLUE Cell products is found in Table 7–4. This table shows that good commercials are likely to be of the Testimonial/Interview, Slice of Life, and Demonstration formats. Conversely, and

Table 7–4
Presence of Message Structure Elements in Good and Poor Radio Commercials— BLUE Cell Products (Proven Recall Only)

Structure Element	Overall (all commercials)	Good (top 37% only)	Poor (bottom 37% only)
Format			
Testimonial	7.0%	8.0%	4.3%
Interview	1.7%	4.0%	1.0%
Slice of Life	24.8%	29.0%	25.0%
Problem Solution	2.0%	0.0%	1.6%
Demonstration	2.0%	3.0%	1.0%
Announcer	62.5%*	56.0%	67.1%
	100.0%	100.0%	100.0%
Mechanical			
60" Length	19.5%*	31.4%	10.7%
Number of Words	94*	103	90
Entry Time	9*	10.3	7.9
No. of Brand Mentions	4	4.3	3.9
Number of Ideas	4.0*	3.9	4.6
No. of Message Reps	3.0	3.0	2.6

*Denotes significant difference between good and poor commercials.

consistent with the correlation values, the Announcer format was found somewhat more often (69.3%) in poor commercials than good commercials (55.8%).

Good commercials also tended to be sixty seconds in length (31.4%) and contained more words (an average of 103). An interesting and important caveat to this finding is that while the longer commercials were associated with good performance, it did not necessarily mean that more ideas led to good performance. It seems that the longer commercials were successful, but cramming too many ideas into these messages did not necessarily produce good performance.

Slice-of-Life Radio Spots Increase Market Share

In January 1992, e.p.t. (Early Pregnancy Test) from Warner Wellcome (previously Warner Lambert) launched an innovative, ear-catching radio campaign and on-air promotion using one test market, Milwaukee, Wisconsin, and one radio station, Contemporary Hit–formatted WKTI FM. Though e.p.t.'s advertising media mix traditionally relied on television, e.p.t. Zone Marketing Manager, Thomas N. McMillian, had always personally believed in radio to effectively target consumers. McMillian's goal with the January 1992 five-week promotion was to raise e.p.t.'s market share by 3%.

To reach the primary demographic of women aged eighteen to thirty-four, J. Walter Thompson, e.p.t.'s advertising agency, developed thirty-second spots using five women's voices and one male voiceover, all asking the same crucial question: "Am I pregnant?" In addition to the thirteen-week radio schedule, e.p.t. worked closely with WKTI to develop a twelve-week, value-added promotion called "The Baby Derby" where radio listeners who were trying to conceive a child were asked to send their stories to the station. The three couples who were eventually chosen were treated to a week in Jamaica to "help things along" and became regulars during WKTI's morning show for twelve weeks to share their progress in becoming parents. The first couple to conceive a child was awarded a number of prizes—including baby furniture, diapers, and scholarship funds—from local Milwaukee vendors. "Listeners were glued to their radios because they enjoyed hearing the updates from the three couples and being a part of their lives during the promotion," said McMillian.

But the radio listeners were not the only ones who enjoyed the promotion. "The results from our radio advertising schedule and promotion were extraordinary," explained McMillian. "e.p.t. sales jumped a full twenty share points—seventeen points above our sales goal! Since radio was the only incremental activity we were doing in Milwaukee, we attribute the entire success of this test to radio."

Due to the huge success in Milwaukee, addition e.p.t. Baby Derbies were held in Chicago and Indianapolis in 1993, and in Dallas in early 1994.[4,5]

Mnemonics Boost Brand Awareness for BLUE Cell Product

In the spring of 1991, radio was added to the media mix of outdoor, transit, and magazines that Listerine in Canada had generally utilized. According to the Senior Media Buyer/Planner at J. Walter Thompson, Listerine's agency, studies had shown that mouthwash users were heavy radio listeners especially in the twelve English markets (including Toronto, Vancouver, Calgary, Edmonton, and Halifax), and at that time, no other competitor was utilizing the medium, ensuring share-of-mind increases. Early-morning drive times allowed Listerine to isolate those times when consumers would be most receptive to the message, and radio enabled Listerine to take a creative risk to revitalize its traditional older-user image.

Three humorous spots, entitled "Polka," "Aria," and "Blues," were produced with gargling sounds accompanying various styles of music. The spots, which targeted adults eighteen to thirty-four and ran for three weeks, communicated the importance of preventing gum disease while making the "rinsing and swishing" sounds a mnemonic device for Listerine.

According to Thompson, radio helped Listerine achieve a +15 share in the market (compared to +7 for the category) on a twelve-month basis due to the strong growth in each region where the spots aired. Additionally, the rinsing and swishing mnemonic device worked so well in radio that it became the focus for the company's "After you brush, Listerine" television campaign. The campaign won a series of radio creative awards including the Marketing Awards and the Crystals.[6] [COMMERCIAL 14 ON DISC]

Presenter Characteristics—BLUE Cell Products

Two presenter characteristics had a positive effect on commercials in the BLUE Cell (see Table 7–5). The number of presenters used in the commercial and messages that incorporated both adult and child presenters led to good performance. The gender of the presenter did not influence performance for commercials in this product category.

When looking at the composite of good and poor radio commercials, an interesting pattern emerges as to which type of presenters tend to work in this product category (Table 7–6). It seems that a mixed aged group of presenters may be the best approach because it is found significantly more often (6.3%) in good commercials than poor (1.0%) commercials. Though not significant, female presenters were found more often in good commercials. However, even though this product category has

Table 7–5
Correlation Between Presenter Characteristics and Discriminant Function—BLUE Cell Products

Presenter Characteristic	Index	Proven	Execution	Persuasion
Adult and Other	+++	+	+++	–
Number of Presenters	+	+++	+++	–

+++, –––, $p \le .05$.

Table 7–6
*Presence of Presenter Characteristics
in Good and Poor Radio Commercials—
BLUE Cell Products (Proven Recall Only)*

Presenter Characteristic	Overall (all commercials)	Good (top 37% only)	Poor (bottom 37%)
Gender			
Male	59.3%*	59.9%	60.7%
Female	9.6%	10.5%	5.7%
Both Together	31.1%	29.7%	33.6%
	100.0%	100.0%	100.0%
Age			
Adult	94.2%	93.0%	99.0%
Teen	1.1%	1.0%	0.0%
Mixed Adult/Other	4.7%*	6.0%	1.0%
	100.0%	100.0%	100.0%
Number of Presenters	2.0*	2.4	2.2

*Denotes significant difference between good and poor commercials.

many items aimed at the female consumer, women were used as presenters less than 10% of the time.

Comedy Group Reaches Shopping Masses

Dixie Value Mall, located west of Toronto, is Canada's largest off-price shopping center, with retail stores like Sears, Winners, and Tip-Top. To help build and maintain awareness and increase the number of shoppers—all while keeping the advertising budget down—mall marketing executives used the creative assistance of Henry Rendall of Toronto-based ad agency Hungadunga, Hungadunga, Hungadunga, Hungadunga, & McCormick. Rendall put together a radio buy of Toronto's top four stations—Adult Contemporary, Easy Listening, Mix, and All News—to reach the target demo of women over twenty-one. The spots created used an important BLUE Cell presenter characteristic of three presenters and an interview format.

Starting in the fall of 1992, three very off-beat bargain hunt-ers, created by Rendall, hit the airwaves with a shopping spree at the Dixie Value Mall. Celebrities from the Second City TV comedy group—Joe Flaherty, Jayne Eastwood, and Don Dickinson—were cast as shoppers, with Derek McGrath as the shoppers' interviewer. The characters describe the shops and inform customers that it's easy to find great buys at the Mall. The fictitious shoppers got the attention of many Toronto radio announcers who talked about them on the air, and as a result, Dixie Value Mall received additional live, on-air exposure.

According to Rendall, "Dixie Value Mall strongly believes in radio because it has always worked well for them. They have received a considerable amount of high praise for the characters and the merchants feel the campaign has increased awareness— and possible shoppers—and enhanced the image of the mall."[7] [COMMERCIAL 15 ON DISC]

A Summary of What Works in the BLUE Cell

The results indicate that very different creative elements work in the BLUE Cell as opposed to the other three product cells. Once again, these differences highlight the importance of using the appropriate creative strategies for different product types. As one might expect, given that these are low-risk products, cues such as mnemonics, related humor, and certain types of music were associated with good performance. Though longer commercials aided in audience recall, those messages that required increased attention, i.e., additional ideas or something new, led to poor performance. This is not surprising, recalling that the audience does not wish to spend a great deal of time thinking about information concerning BLUE Cell products. Also, once again the Announcer format did not lead to good performance.

Though not used very often (only 30% of the time), commercials that incorporated related humor performed particularly well. It could be that the low-risk nature of these products allows for a more "light-hearted appeal." This strategy is particularly interesting in light of the fact that those commercials that did not use any type of humor performed rather poorly.

	Worked Well	Did Not Work Well
All Commercial Measures	Functional mnemonics Non-functional mnemonics More brand mentions More presenters	No mnemonics Something new Too many ideas Announcer format
Proven Recall	60" length More words Later brand entry Fewer ideas Mixed age presenters (adults and others) Related humor Female presenters	No humor No music Other music

Figure 7–1

What Works and Doesn't Work in the BLUE Cell

Music had an interesting impact on performance. Most commercials (40.6%) either did not use music or included it as other or background music (37.8%). However, these elements were strongly associated with poor commercial recall. Overall, it seems that music had little positive effect on performance in this cell. The low-risk serious factors associated with these products indicate that other peripheral cues may be more effective and should be considered as alternative tactics.

There is strong evidence that mnemonics work well in this cell. Though used slightly less often (combined, 41.8% of the time), commercials that incorporated either a functional or non-functional mnemonic performed better than those in which no mnemonic was included. The reader will recall that the low-risk nature of these products leads to less audience attention and cognitive processing. Hence, creative tactics, such as mnemonic devices, can overcome the low audience attention span and allow for easier cognitive processing of the commercial message. Once again, the Announcer format was the most popular format, used in 62.5% of the commercials in this cell. Additionally, there is evidence that this tactic is associated most often with poor performance.

Finally, even though the nature of the products in this category would seem to call for the increased use of women or both men and women as presenters, relatively few commercials took this approach, despite the tendency for female presenters to have a positive impact on commercial performance.

The results give continued evidence that recall and commercial performance are strongly influenced by commercial length. Commercials that were longer, had more brand mentions, and more words performed well. Curiously, over 80% of the commercials in this cell were thirty-second spots. One wonders if budgetary constraints led to the decision to use shorter commercials. If this is the case, the overall sacrifice may not be worth the few dollars saved.

The results discussed in this chapter strongly suggest that some of the current practices being used in BLUE Cell radio commercials should be reexamined. The information indicates that many of these tactics lead to a less than optimal performance. Conversely, the tactics used less often seem to be the ones that lead to better commercial performance.

Chapter 8

Anatomy of a Good Commercial for Low-Risk Toys— YELLOW Cell Products

It is far easier to write ten passably effective Sonnets, good enough to take in the not too inquiring critic, than one effective advertisement that will take in a few thousand of the uncritical buying public.

—*Aldous Huxley in* On the Margin

T he final product category in the analysis includes the low-risk little treats or toys. Identified as YELLOW Cell products, these goods provide the small day-to-day rewards. They are products that are routinely purchased but also generate a small emotional response. Items in this category include snack foods, desserts, and alcoholic beverages.

Structurally, commercials in the YELLOW Cell:

- mostly do not use humor, but more than any other products
- mostly use some form of music
- mostly use radio sound
- show an almost even split between including functional mnemonics or excluding mnemonics entirely
- show the highest use of Something New

- show heavy use of the Announcer format
- mostly use thirty-second spots
- tend to use male-only presenters
- though most commercials use Adult presenters, this cell shows the highest use of teenagers as presenters

What Works in the YELLOW Cell

Yellow Cell products are of relatively low risk and routinely purchased. Based on this, we would expect consumers to pay little attention to commercial content. However, the fact that these products are also small rewards provides an opportunity to engage listeners with peripheral cues such as music and humor.

Message Style Elements—YELLOW Cell Products

A relatively large number of message style creative elements influenced commercial performance in this product category (Table 8–1). Elements such as Related Humor, TV Version, Re-

Table 8–1

Correlation Between Message Style Elements and Discriminant Function—YELLOW Cell Products

Style Element	Index	Proven	Execution	Persuasion
Related Audio	+++	+++	+++	−
Functional Mnemonics	+++	+++	+	−
Jingle Music	+++	+++	+	−
TV Version	+	+	+++	+++
Related Humor	+	+++	+++	+++
Singing Music	−−−	−−−	−−−	−
Unrelated Humor	−−−	−−−	−	−−−
Something New	−−−	−−−	−−−	+
No Mnemonics	−−−	−−−	−	+
Non-functional Mnemonics	−−−	−−−	−	+++

+++, −−−, $p \le .05$.
+, −, $p > .05$.

lated Audio, Functional Mnemonics, and Jingles all had a positive relationship with the communication index, proven, and
execution recall. However, only Related Humor and TV Version had a positive correlation with persuasion. By contrast, Unrelated Humor, Singing Music, Something New, No Mnemonics, and Non-functional Mnemonics had a negative relationship
with the response measures. Interestingly, Something New, No
Mnemonics, and Non-functional Mnemonics had a positive effect on persuasion.

The composite profile shows that while Related Humor is
used in only 23% of the commercials, it does tend to contribute
to good performance; almost 28% of the good commercials
used this style element (Table 8–2). On the other hand, Unrelated Humor (though used less often) was found more often
(21.4%) in poor commercials.

The use of music appears to be a popular creative element for
YELLOW Cell products. Combined, over 75% of the commercials for YELLOW Cell products included some type of music.
Though music had a strong representation in this product category, the various styles had a diverse effect on performance. Jingles were found more commonly in good commercials (34.2%)
than in poor commercials (20%). Conversely, Singing Music
appeared to have a negative effect. This style was found twice as
often in poor commercials (27.1%) as in good commercials
(13.3%). Other music was equally associated with poor commercials.

For the first time, the use of Related Audio was associated
with good commercials. This popular approach was used in
77.4% of the commercials and was found more often in good
(84.5%) than in poor commercials (63.6%). Though not statistically significant, Unrelated Audio was present more often in
poor commercials. These results suggest that the current strategy of using Related Audio and avoiding the Unrelated style
may be the best bet for YELLOW Cell product ads.

The origin of the commercial and the use of Mnemonics also
had an interesting effect on commercial performance. Though
used in only 7.6% of the commercials for YELLOW Cell prod-

Table 8–2
*Presence of Message Style Elements
in Good and Poor Radio Commercials—
YELLOW Cell Products (Proven Recall Only)*

Style Element	Overall (%) (all commercials)	Good (%) (top 37% only)	Poor (%) (bottom 37% only)
Humor			
No Humor	58.9	59.9	61.5
Related Humor	23.0*	27.8	17.1
Unrelated Humor	18.1	12.3	21.4
	100.0	100.0	100.0
Music			
No Music	23.4	21.9	22.9
Jingles	28.3*	34.2	20.0
Singing Music	19.4*	13.3	27.1
Other Music	28.9	30.6	30.0
	100.0	100.0	100.0
Audio			
Related Audio	77.4*	84.5	63.6
Unrelated Audio	22.6	15.5	36.4
	100.0	100.0	100.0
Commercial Origin			
TV Sound	0.0	0.0	0.0
TV Version	7.6*	9.6	4.2
Radio Sound	92.4	90.4	95.8
	100.0	100.0	100.0
Mnemonics			
No Mnemonics	50.5*	42.2	63.0
Functional	46.0*	57.8	31.0
Non-functional	3.5*	0.0	6.0
Fantasy	0.0	0.0	0.0
	100.0	100.0	100.0
Something New	19.6	13.9	22.9

*Denotes significant difference between good and poor commercials.

ucts, the TV Version was more than twice as likely to be found in good commercials (9.6%) as in poor commercials (4.2%). Also, almost half of the commercials in this product category used some sort of mnemonic device. The use of functional mnemonics seemed to lead to better performance as they were found in almost 58% of the good commercials while appearing in only 30.7% of the poor commercials. Commercials that did not use a mnemonic device or tried the non-functional mnemonic approach tended to perform poorly.

Functional Mnemonics Increase Awareness of Freixenet Sparkling Wine

Freixenet (pronounced Fresh-i-net) was introduced in the United States in the late 1970s with, initially, a television-driven advertising campaign. However, as the years passed, escalating media costs were rising faster than profits and Freixenet turned to cost-effective radio to reach its target of well-educated urban professionals, twenty-four to thirty-five years of age. Freixenet's challenges were to overcome the obstacle of a name that is difficult to pronounce, and to communicate the product's superior quality and its strikingly distinct black bottle.

In 1987, Freixenet enlisted the help of the radio creative team of Bert Berdis & Co. to develop a humorous campaign playing off the confusion consumers have with the unusual Freixenet name. The concept became "The Black Bottle Bubbly" campaign, capitalizing on the brand's unique black bottle and leaving a strong, memorable visual image with listeners. The Freixenet campaign runs on a variety of national stations and formats: "We look at programming that might appeal to women, but we also want to balance that out with the stations that attract male listeners," explained Freixenet USA Director of Communications Sydney Randazzo.

"In radio, we are able to make a stronger presence and essentially own the medium," said Randazzo. "Radio allows us to get more messages across to reach and motivate consumers. A lot of impressions are made on people driving home or to work—hopefully, they'll stop in a store on the way home and purchase a bottle of Freixenet. We've received great feedback from our field managers—the radio ads have certainly created more awareness of our product!" And while television is still a part of Freixenet's media mix, the company continues to devote a large portion of its advertising budget to radio.[1,2] [COMMERCIALS 16–19 ON DISC]

Twelve Refreshing Messages and Contemporary Jingle Sell New Canadian Beverage

Sting is an alcoholic "refresher" available in Ontario, Canada in three flavors: Long Island Iced Tea, Vodka Stingers, and Tequila Lime. Positioned against both wine coolers and beer, Sting was launched throughout the province of Ontario exclusively on radio in the summer of 1993 because, according to Richard Truman, President and Director of Creative Services of the Campaign House, Sting's advertising agency for this campaign, "radio is the ideal summer medium to reach our primary target audience of Generation X—the 1.5 million adults in Ontario between the ages of nineteen and twenty-nine—and our secondary target of adults twenty-nine to thirty-five who enjoy entertaining in the summer months. Radio also allowed us to create twelve different messages at a fraction of the cost of TV."

Campaign House recorded six spots with a female voice and six spots with a male voice with all twelve closing with the phrase "don't go where you've been." A contemporary music bed helped communicate the "hip" image of the beverage. "Because of radio, Sting is now an established brand in Ontario and sales have exceeded our forecast numbers," said Truman.[3] [COMMERCIAL 20 ON DISC]

Catchy Jingle Wins Pizza War

Using radio with jingles and an easy-to-remember phone number phrase, Pizza Hut in Atlanta was able to completely reverse its position in the Atlanta pizza delivery market. In 1989, to dominate delivery, Pizza Hut needed to increase the top-of-mind awareness that Domino's Pizza owned with a seventy-two to twenty-seven advantage. Pizza Hut invested heavily in mass print and radio to leverage and extend their television advertising. The initial radio campaign featured the voice of Garfield, the popular cartoon cat, in the role of a loyal Pizza Hut Delivery person who couldn't wait to tell the listeners about Pizza Hut's latest deal. Garfield's personal, entertaining, and informative message was sandwiched between a music bed that featured Pizza Hut's one-number jingle: "When it's gotta be hot, we're ready to drive. Call 662–5555."

Pizza Hut updated its campaign in 1992 to carry specific promotional messages to two primary targets: men eighteen to thirty-four and working women with children. The new "Hotlanta's Calling Pizza Hut Tonite" utilizes a man and a woman who speak directly to the split target, while a foot-tapping pop/dance song plays in the background.

According to Brian J. Hunt, Marketing Director, Pizza Hut, Inc./Georgia Market, "We have been the only pizza competitor in Atlanta to consistently utilize local radio since 1989 because radio enabled us to optimize reach and frequency and watch our top-of-mind awareness, sales, and share grow! Our 1992 campaign gave us a 50 to 20 share advantage over Domino's Pizza—a swing of over 25 points in a $200 million pizza market—and we grabbed the top-of-mind awareness leadership position by a 52 to 38 advantage. And, our delivery share advantage over Domino's is now 59 to 34—a complete reversal from the 59 to 27 advantage that Domino's held in 1989."[4,5]

Message Structure Elements—YELLOW Cell Products

In the message structure category, three elements had a positive influence and two had a negative influence on the performance of YELLOW Cell product ads (Table 8–3). The Slice of Life Format, the number of Message Repetitions, and the number of times the brand was mentioned all contributed to good commercial performance. Hence, the more often the message was

Table 8–3

*Correlation Between Message Structure Elements
and Discriminant Function—YELLOW Cell Products*

Structure Element	Index	Proven	Execution	Persuasion
Number of Message Reps	+++	+++	+++	---
Number of Mentions	+++	+++	+	---
Slice of Life Format	+	+	+++	+
Announcer Format	–	---	---	–
Number of Ideas	---	---	---	+++

+++, ---, $p \le .05$.
+, –, $p > .05$.

repeated and the more times the brand was identified, the better the communication index, proven, and execution recall. However, this did not always translate to increased persuasion. The number of message repetitions and the number of times the brand name was mentioned had a negative correlation with persuasion.

Generally, both the Announcer format and the Number of Ideas were negatively related to performance. Given, the emotional, and at times fun, aspect associated with YELLOW Cell products, it is not surprising that the serious Announcer format would not perform well. Also, the routine purchase behavior of this type of product would make the increased number of ideas less proficient.

The profile of good and poor commercials shown in Table 8–4 indicates that the Slice of Life format was the most commonly used structural format in good commercials. This format appeared in almost 30% of the good commercials while being present in only 21.5% of the poor commercials. Interestingly, the Announcer format, which was the most heavily used structural format (61%), was associated more often with poor commercials (70.7%) than good commercials (57.8%). It may be that the Announcer format has been used too often and is not necessarily the best approach for YELLOW Cell products.

Table 8–4
Presence of Message Structure Elements
in Good and Poor Radio Commercials—
YELLOW Cell Products (Proven Recall Only)

Structure Element	Overall (all commercials)	Good (top 37% only)	Poor (bottom 37% only)
Format			
Testimonial	6.0%	8.2%	5.1%
Interview	1.0%	1.0%	0.0%
Slice of Life	29.2%*	29.9%	21.4%
Problem Solution	1.0%	1.0%	1.4%
Demonstration	1.8%	2.1%	1.4%
Announcer	61.0%*	57.8%	70.7%
	100.0%	100.0%	100.0%
Mechanical			
60" Length	38.6%*	42.2%	32.9%
Number of Words	103	107	100
Entry Time	8	8	9.1
No. of Brand Mentions	5*	5.6	4.8
Number of Ideas	4*	4.0	4.5
No. of Message Reps	3*	3.8	3.2

*Denotes significant difference between good and poor commercials.

Though not significantly correlated with performance, there is some evidence that message length and the number of words in the commercial contribute to improved performance. A larger proportion (42.4%) of the good commercials were sixty seconds in length as opposed to only 32.9% of the poor commercials. Also, on the average, good commercials tended to have more words (107) than poor commercials (100). However, the negative effect of too many ideas in the message is consistent with the results found in the other low-risk cell (BLUE) and in direct contrast with the findings in the high-risk WHITE and RED Cells. Commercials that included more ideas worked better for high- than for low-risk products. This information lends support to the idea that consumers will not be receptive to excess information for products that are routinely purchased but are willing to accept information for high-risk products that demand a more involved decision process.

Slice of Life Radio Spots Capture Market for Molson Breweries USA

A popular radio campaign that has captured the imagination of millions of Americans since 1983 has enabled Molson Beer and Ale sales to continue to increase steadily with a growth rate of 6% in a beer consumption market that is flat to down overall. And Molson, the second largest volume importer in the country, ranks as the number one Canadian beer in the United States. Molson's Director of Marketing, Peter Reaske, has relied heavily on radio since 1983 because the medium has proven so successful. "The initial decision to use radio was spurred by its ability to really hit our target audience—men from legal drinking age through thirty-four in the medium- to high-income bracket," explained Reaske.

The special male/female chemistry captured in each Molson spot is credited to the campaign creators and voices—Ann Winn and Garrett Brown—whose work has been widely imitated since the first Molson spot, "Border," aired in twenty markets in 1983. That same ad, and twenty-two others, ran in cities across the United States for nearly a decade.

"When consumers in focus groups are asked to recall beer ad campaigns, Molson is just as likely to appear in the top five brands that spend millions on their advertising," said Reaske. "Our share of mind is tremendous in light of what we spend. Radio allows us to command a significant share of voice in an affordable medium."[6,7] [COMMERCIALS 21–24 ON DISC]

Presenter Characteristics—YELLOW Cell Products

Two presenter characteristics had a positive correlation with performance and one had a negative effect on commercials for

Table 8–5

*Correlation Between Presenter Characteristics
and Discriminant Function—YELLOW Cell Products*

Presenter Characteristic	Index	Proven	Execution	Persuasion
Female	+++	+++	+++	–
Adult and Other	+	+++	+++	+++
Number of Presenters	– – –	– – –	– – –	–

+++, – – –, $p \leq .05$.
+, –, $p > .05$.

YELLOW Cell products (Table 8–5). The use of Mixed-Age presenters and Female presenters had a positive impact on performance, while the number of presenters had a negative influence. The use of Mixed-Aged presenters was also significant for BLUE Cell commercials, giving some indication that this presenter tactic may be useful for low-risk products. Interestingly, this was the only category where the use of Female presenters influenced performance. However, although Female presenters led to a better communication index, proven, and execution recall, they had a slightly negative effect on persuasion. Also, the negative correlation associated with the number of presenters mirrors its impact with the other experiential product cell (the RED Cell). Having too many presenters may not be a good idea for toy-type products.

A fuller picture is developed when Table 8–6 is examined. This table shows that while Male presenters are used most often (58.0%), they are more likely to be found in poor commercials (65.7%) than in good commercials (57.2%). Once again, Female presenters are used infrequently (7.3%) even though they are more often associated with good (13.3%) rather than poor commercials (3.6%). Finally, even though Mixed-Age presenters show a positive correlation and are more likely to appear in good (6.4%) rather than poor (1.0%) commercials, they are seldom used (3.6%).

Table 8–6

*Presence of Presenter Characteristics
in Good and Poor Radio Commercials—
YELLOW Cell Products (Proven Recall Only)*

Presenter Characteristic	Overall (all commercials)	Good (top 37% only)	Poor (bottom 37% only)
Gender			
Male	58.0%	57.3%	65.7%
Female	7.3%*	13.3%	3.6%
Both Together	34.7%	29.4%	30.7%
	100.0%	100.0%	100.0%
Age			
Adult	92.3%	89.3%	93.3%
Teen	4.3%	4.3%	5.7%
Mixed Adult/Other	3.6%	6.4%	1.0%
	100.0%	100.0%	100.0%
Number of Presenters	3.0*	6.4	1.0

*Denotes significant difference between good and poor commercials.

Humor Sells Laughing Cow Cheeses

In 1983, with a relatively small advertising budget of $375,000, Fromageries Bel needed a cost-efficient way to introduce its new product: the Laughing Cow brand of mini-cheeses packaged in the "distinctive red net bags" that are the perfect snack food for any time. Fromageries Bell President Frank Schnieders was looking for a one-time 25% incremental sales gain in the New York market. A thirteen-week, New York metro area, radio-only campaign was put together by TBWA Advertising with the creative assistance of Joy Golden, President of Joy Radio, a New York City–based radio creative house. Golden recruited character voice artists Lynn Lipton and Julie Cohen to breathe life into a series of scripts revolving around "five little laughing cows in a red net bag." Lipton, as the now famous heavily ac-cented New Yorker, and Cohen, as the quintessential California Valley Girl, became the voices of Laughing Cow mini-cheeses until the campaign ended in 1987.

During the initial thirteen-week cycle—which ran on nearly every radio station in the New York City area—New York sales skyrocketed with a 62% increase. This success convinced Fromageries Bel to expand the humorous, radio-only campaign to eleven additional cities. According to Golden, when the campaign hit Los Angeles, sales jumped 95%; San Francisco experienced an immediate 125% jump in sales; and stores in Boston, Philadelphia, and Miami sold out of Laughing Cow. During the four-year campaign, overall sales jumped 52% nationwide.[8,9] [COMMERCIALS 25–26 ON DISC]

Summary of What Works in the YELLOW Cell

This chapter looked at the structure of commercials for the low-risk toys, i.e., YELLOW Cell products. The results show that a number of style factors had a positive influence on commercials in this cell. These include such elements as Related Humor, Jingles, and Functional Mnemonics. However, the prospect of including Something New in the commercial led to poorer performance. Once again, longer commercials led to better recall. However, while an increase in the number of ideas inhibited comprehension and recall, it did have a positive impact on persuasion. Additionally, the Announcer format did not perform well, but the Slice of Life format did tend to lead to better performance. Though it is overshadowed by the extensive use of commercials made specifically for radio, there is evidence that the TV version style may be an effective strategy in this cell. This cell also shows the heaviest use of female-only presenters and they appeared to have had a very positive impact on performance.

The more emotional stimulating styles of humor and music seem to blend well with the low-risk toys. Given that the audience will devote little attention to these commercials, a somewhat more emotional approach seems to fit well with the experiential aspects of the product. Consumers will use these elements as peripheral cues in evaluating the product and the commercial. Also, the low attention paid to these commercials makes the functional mnemonic element a valuable tactic. Again, the audience will process some information if it is relatively easy to assimilate. However, when more extensive thought is required, such as Something New in the commercial, there is a tendency to avoid or reject this additional information.

The Slice of Life format seems to work well in this cell. This may be due to the experiential connection associated with these products. The audience may also be able to better relate to these commercials and sense a connection with their own life experiences. This may also help explain the negative effects of the Announcer format where the audience may find it difficult to establish an association with the Announcer and events in their own lives.

As with the BLUE Cell commercials, the more often a message was repeated and the more times the brand was mentioned, the stronger the communication index, proven and execution

	Worked Well	Did Not Work Well
All Commercial Measures	Related humor TV version Mixed age presenters (adult and other) Age presenters	Unrelated humor Singing music Unrelated audio Announcer format Too many presenters
Proven Recall	Jingles Related audio Functional mnemonics Slice of life format 60" length More brand mentions More repetitions Female presenters	Something new No mnemonics Non-functional mnemonics More ideas

Figure 8–1

What Works and Doesn't Work in the YELLOW Cell

recall. Increased exposure will act as a peripheral cue when the more times one is exposed to the message, the more it will influence recall and attitudes. This is done with relatively little thought about commercial content and the information provided. This also explains why commercials tended to have poorer performance when more ideas were included. The audience is not willing to process and think about information content and will reject it "out of hand."

Additional presenters appear to have had a strong positive influence on performance. The audience may use the number of presenters as a peripheral cue, and rather than process information, they will make a judgment based on a consensus of sources. Though commercials in this category were dominated by Male presenters, this was also the only cell where we were able to judge the impact of female presenters. Overall, Female presenters had a strong positive effect on commercial performance. Once again, the question arises as to why a creative tactic that leads to good performance is often avoided. The results suggest that many radio advertisers need to rethink their creative approaches when constructing commercials for YELLOW Cell products.

Chapter 9

Epilogue

No prediction of radio's future can be so wild, so fantastic, that even the most unimaginative engineer will dismiss it as impossible of realization.

—Waldemar Kaempffert
in The Popular History of American Invention

The successful ads examined in this book and heard on its companion disc make it clear that radio is a highly effective advertising medium that can market products ranging from shoes to cars to law services. As the center of a media plan or in a supporting role, radio works hard to make money for its advertisers. And in this era when advertising costs are sky high, competition is fierce, customers are getting immune to traditional advertising, and ad budgets are tight, the time is right for clever advertisers to capitalize on radio. As the ultimate niche marketing medium, radio inexpensively and creatively communicates with the consumers advertisers need to reach to buy their products and increase their bottom-line profits.

But as noted, despite radio's extensive reach, frequency, precise targeting capabilities, unlimited creative opportunities, and relatively low production and air-time costs, far too few companies in the United States and Canada effectively utilize radio today. Likewise, a surprising number of companies choose to "ignore" radio, while others take advantage of just a few of its inherent strengths. In essence, radio continues to be caught in a vicious cycle of some agencies not recommending radio to their clients, while clients are hesitant to suggest using the medium to their agencies because they may be completely unfamiliar with radio's attributes and successful track record. We hope that this book has provided agency personnel responsible for media planning, buying, and creative with some tangible advice about how to easily and effectively add successful radio campaigns to their list of credentials. Subsequently, we hope that advertisers will begin asking their agencies to consider radio as a significant part of their media package. The smart advertisers who move into radio fast will be able to dominate the airwaves with only a modest reallocation of their media dollars.

On the Technological Front

There are plenty of reasons why more advertisers and agencies should get on the fast track and invest in radio advertising. With all the country abuzz about the electronic superhighway, radio can easily be the first to pay the toll and speed along. David Alwadish, a New York-based entrepreneur, is currently marketing his patented "CouponRadio™," a new product that utilizes Radio Broadcast Data System (RBDS). RBDS is a portion of the FM radio signal that can be digitally converted into brief messages—like a radio station's call letters, song titles and artists, traffic directions, and electronic coupons. Using a special car radio receiver, if a listener hears an ad for a $200 rebate at a local auto dealer, for example, he or she simply inserts Alwadish's "RadioCard™" into the receiver and the coupon is recorded onto the card's microchip. The listener then takes the credit-card-sized RadioCard to the participating dealer, who prints out and honors the coupon. And, because the date, time, and radio station where the ad was heard are recorded onto the RadioCard, advertisers are provided with immediate proof that their ads are effectively reaching their target audience.

In another scenario, if a listener wishes to know the song title and artist of a particular song, he or she can punch a button on the receiver and the station broadcasting the song will digitally send the information to the listener's receiver. The listener can then retrieve the information, which is displayed on the receiver's sixty-four-character LCD screen, at a convenient time, or record the information on his or her RadioCard, and take the card to a participating record store that will print out the songs and artists heard for the listener to use as a shopping list. When the RadioCard is used in this manner, the participating record shop also prints out discount coupons that can be used toward store purchases. Or, all information can be displayed as soon as it is heard by the listener, saved, and re-displayed at a later time.

According to Alwadish, "CouponRadio greatly enhances the effectiveness of radio for advertisers. If a listener is driving at sixty miles an hour and hears an ad for a retail store that he is interested in visiting, he can't stop the car and jot down the phone number or location. This technology allows him to record the advertiser's name, number, and location onto his RadioCard and shop at the retailer at a convenient time. In turn, this greatly helps increase awareness and store traffic for advertisers. And that translates to bigger advertiser profits."

On the audio/technological side, the National Radio Systems Committee and the Electronic Industries Association have formed the Digital Audio Radio (DAR) Subcommittee to work together to greatly enhance radio's sound quality and increase the frequency range of stations across the United States. The DAR, representing broadcasters from the National Association of Broadcasters and members of the electronics industry, is testing five terrestrial transmission systems at the NASA Lewis Research Center in Cleveland. Following the testing, a standard is expected to be chosen in 1995. Radio broadcasters already have a preference for one of the systems currently in testing—In-Band On Channel—which places a digital signal on top of the current analog signal used throughout the radio broadcasting industry. If approved, the In-Band system, broadcasters say, will cause minimal equipment and frequency disruption: that's good news for consumers, who won't be faced with cost-prohibitive receivers, and for radio stations, who need only a device called a "digital exciter" to broadcast to radios across the country. The good news for advertisers is that more listeners in expanded listening areas can hear their messages without the fear of interference due to weak signals.

Some Final Words

Although radio advertising has existed for more than seventy years, in many ways we are entering its most exciting and lucrative period. With the various technological enhancements about to become everyday realities, there is simply no reason why radio cannot play on the same field with television or cable TV. With solid planning, ingenuity, and the information contained in this book, advertisers can be well prepared to broadcast *winning* messages to the *right* audiences to meet sales goals and stay within budget.

While there are no magic, all-purpose radio strategies, the information in this book makes it clear that some tactics work better for certain categories of products than others. Copywriters and creative directors now have some hard data to save them from airing ads that have little chance of increasing sales. Most experienced advertising professionals would know intuitively that humor is not likely to be effective in selling law services or life insurance, but might have less feel for whether testimonials help to sell sports cars, or if an announcer will be effective in a spot for beer. Though no inviolate golden rules of advertising have now or are likely to be uncovered, revealing the odds of success with different commercial features is a significant advance in the field of radio advertising where little objective guidance exists. Now, advertisers and their agencies can benefit from the experience gained in the over 2,000 ads examined to write this book.

And because many media experts, like Veronis, Suhler & Associates,[1] expect radio revenue to break the $10 billion mark in 1995, the time is now for agencies and their client advertisers to discover what works and what doesn't work in marketing their products. Cost-efficiency and unique niche marketing capabilities aside, radio's unlimited creative abilities are what will make it shine well throughout the next century.

Appendix A

Radio Recall Research, Inc. Method and Response Measures

Commercial Exposure and Sample

Radio Recall Research, Inc. employs a semi-forced off-air method for testing commercials. Each test commercial is exposed to subjects recruited in shopping malls to fit the audience profile defined by the client firms. Each test ad is edited to be placed between two non-test radio ads, and the pod is placed in the context of background radio playing with music appropriate to the audience being tested. While subjects in a room at the mall location are busy at another task, the radio with the test ad is playing in the background. Approximately 200 individuals at three locations are exposed to each radio ad. Typically, the individuals recruited are, at client specification, characteristic of the current or potential users of the product category represented in the commercial. The sample ads represent dozens of product categories and hundreds of brands. Each ad is coded by the company for dozens of characteristics that might plausibly affect response. The features used in the analysis for this book are indicated in Appendix B.

Consumers are contacted by telephone the next day after exposure to the radio ads using the following protocol.

1. While you were being interviewed yesterday, do you recall hearing a radio playing? (If no, terminate interview)
2. What product or service did you hear advertised on the radio that was playing during yesterday's interview? (*Unaided Brand Recall*—if the test brand is identified, skip to question 5)
3. Do you recall a commercial for (product category for the test product, for example a pain reliever or a soft drink)? (*Category-Aided Brand Recall*)
4. Do you recall hearing a commercial for (test brand)? (If yes, *Claimed Recall*; if no, terminate interview.)
5. You said you remember hearing a commercial for (test brand):
   A. Please describe what you heard during that commercial. What else (prompt)? Anything else (second prompt)? (*Execution and/or Proven Recall*)
   B. What did the commercial say about the brand? Anything else (prompt)? (*Message Recall*)
   C. What ideas about the (test brand) did you get from the commercial? Any other (prompt)? (*Message Recall*)
   D. What thoughts went through your mind when you heard the commercial? (*Message Recall*)

Proven Recall. Verbatim testimony that contains either playback of a specific element in the commercial, even if accompanied by incorrect testimony, or playback of a general element presented in the commercial with nothing incorrect being mentioned.

Message Recall. Some specific, and correct, playback of a sales element in the commercial.

Execution Recall. A specific, and correct, identification of the type of commercial execution (an announcer, a jingle, act of a slice-of-life, and so forth).

Persuasion. A pre-post measure of purchase intention taken before exposure to radio ads and after the ads but before the consumer leaves the mall exposure setting.

These measures represent an array of remembering related and unrelated to the product and with or without prompting. In fact, in relation to the Advertising Research Foundation (ARF) study, these so-called recall measures are really a blend of recall, communication, and comprehension. Unaided Brand Recall, Category-Aided Recall, and Claimed Recall correspond to three recall measures tested by ARF. Of the three, the first, Unaided Brand Recall, outperformed the others and was able to predict sales 87% of the time.

Proven, Message, and Execution Recall correspond to the measures labeled communication in the ARF study. Of the three, Proven Recall (main point communication) and Execution Recall (ad situation/visual) performed particularly well. Recall of key copy points—Message Recall—has even been granted the status of a "comprehension" rather than a recall measure by some researchers.[1]

Sewall and Sarel[2] found that the six recall measures used by Radio Recall Research, Inc. were very highly intercorrelated. In this book the first five recall measures listed above were most highly intercorrelated (Cronbach's alpha of .93). When a composite index of the first five recall variables was developed, the individual item correlation ranged from .86 (brand recall) to .93 (claimed recall). The creation of this "Communication Index" out of the five individual measures was designed to provide a more reliable indicator of the recall/communication/comprehension construct than any one variable by itself could provide. Execution Recall correlated in the .6 to .7 range with the other recall variables and it was used as a separate measure of ad performance. Proven Recall, though also part of the Communication Index, is reported separately because of its high regard by practitioners and the positive correlation with sales found in the ARF study.

Persuasion is a variable created in this study by substracting

the pre-exposure purchase intention expressed by consumers
from their post radio ad exposure purchase intention scores.
Both measures are obtained from respondents before they leave
the mall setting. Persuasion here refers to the change in purchase
intent as expressed as a percentage from 0 to 100. The range of
change in pre- and post-exposure persuasion for the whole sample is from −65% to + 62% with a mean of 2.5%. This means
that some consumers' purchase intentions rose and some declined after hearing the radio ads.

The combination of the Communication Index, Proven Recall, Execution Recall, and Persuasion provides an array of
ways to evaluate the success of the radio ads in the sample. The
relationships among the communication index, execution recall, proven recall, and persuasion vary considerably. As might
be expected, the correlations among the measures range from
.64 to .95 (see Appendix C). Persuasion does not correlate well.
For WHITE, BLUE, and YELLOW goods the correlations are
positive but range from .02 to .47. Persuasion correlates the
least with executional recall and best with the communication
index. For RED goods persuasion is negatively correlated with
the other three variables. Though it would be ideal to have
stronger correlations with persuasion, the strength of the correlation among the other three measures is perhaps more important. Based on Haley's work for ARF benchmarking advertising
response measures against actual sales performance, persuasion
measures as a class were not as predictive as the better re-
call/communication measures.

Appendix B
Coded Commercial Features Used

Message Style

Something new

None

New improvement, new use, new product, new package, new features emphasized

Humor

No humor—no intent to be humorous as judged by client

Related Humor—coded by client indicating *intent* to be humorous with *a function*

Unrelated Humor—coded by client indicating *intent* to be humorous for *attention only*

Music

No music

Jingles—part of primary format

Singing Music—part of sing and sell

Other Music—including music whose function is message, setting background, mnemonic, or mood

Sound Effects	None
	Related Audio
	Unrelated Audio
Commercial Origin	TV Soundtrack
	Radio Execution of TV Version
	Radio Sound only
Slogan/Mneumonics	None
	Functional
	Non-functional
	Fantasy

Message Structure

Execution Format	Testimonial—none or real/staged
	Interview
	Slice of Life
	Problem Solution
	Demonstration
	Announcer talking
Length	30 seconds
	60 seconds
Number of Words	Coded in units of 15 from 36–50 to 171+
Brand Entry Time	Coded in units of 5 seconds from 0–5 to 46+
Number of Brand Mentions	Coded actual number for 1 to 10+
Number of Product Ideas	Coded actual number 1 to 10+
Number of Major Message Repetitions	Coded actual number 1 to 10+

Major Presenters

Number of Major Presenters	Coded actual number from 1 to 6+/chorus

Sex of Presenter(s)	Man alone
	Woman alone
	Both man and woman alone
Age of Presenter(s)	Adult
	Teen
	Adult and other (with teen and/or child)

Radio Recall Research, Inc. codes other commercial features. However, preliminary analysis indicated that frequencies were too low for some features to be included in the analysis of this book.

Appendix C
Correlations Among Measures

Table C–1
Correlation Among Dependent Measures for WHITE Goods

	Execution Recall	Proven Recall	Communication Index	Persuasion
Execution Recall	1.0	.80	.76	0.8
Proven Recall		1.0	.95	.44
Communication Index			1.0	.47
Persuasion				1.0

Table C–2
Correlation Among Dependent Measures for RED Goods

	Execution Recall	Proven Recall	Communication Index	Persuasion
Execution Recall	1.0	.72	.64	−.12
Proven Recall		1.0	.90	−.01
Communication Index			1.0	.05
Persuasion				1.0

Table C–3

Correlation Among Dependent Measures for BLUE Goods

	Execution Recall	Proven Recall	Communication Index	Persuasion
Execution Recall	1.0	.73	.64	.12
Proven Recall		1.0	.89	.14
Communication Index			1.0	.18
Persuasion				1.0

Table C–4

Correlation Among Dependent Measures for YELLOW Goods

	Execution Recall	Proven Recall	Communication Index	Persuasion
Execution Recall	1.0	.83	.78	.02
Proven Recall		1.0	.90	.03
Communication Index			1.0	.09
Persuasion				1.0

Table C–5

Correlation Among Dependent Measures for All Products Combined

	Execution Recall	Proven Recall	Communication Index	Persuasion
Execution Recall	1.0	.79	.72	.05
Proven Recall		1.0	.90	.14
Communication Index			1.0	.19
Persuasion				1.0

Appendix D
Classification Rates from Discriminant Analysis

Table D-1

Discriminant Classification Percentages—WHITE Goods

	Execution	Proven	Communication Index	Persuasion
Cannonical Correlation	.99	.84	.81	.93
Chi-Square Significance	.000	.000	.000	.000
Model 60% % Correctly Classified				
Poor Performing	100.0%	91.7%	92.2%	100.0%
Ads	(12)	(84)	(59)	(23)
Good Performing	100.0%	90.3%	91.9%	100.0%
Ads	(21)	(62)	(34)	(26)
Holdout 40% % Correctly Classified:				
Poor Performing	56.3%	88.9%	92.3%	91.7%
Ads	(9)	(48)	(24)	(11)
Good Performing	100.0%	90.0%	92.0%	90.5%
Ads	(13)	(36)	(26)	(19)

Table D–2

Discriminant Classification Percentages—RED Goods

	Execution	Proven	Communi-cation Index	Persuasion
Cannonical Correlation	.95	.77	.92	.78
Chi-Square Significance	.000	.001	.000	.086
Model 60% % Correctly Classified				
Poor Performing Ads	100.0% (11)	85.7% (24)	100.0% (20)	94.4% (34)
Good Performing Ads	100.0% (19)	93.3% (42)	97.8% (45)	70.0% (7)
Holdout 40% % Correctly Classified:				
Poor Performing Ads	85.7% (6)	66.7% (4)	100.0% (7)	81.0% (17)
Good Performing Ads	100.0% (38)	85.0% (34)	92.9% (26)	83.3% (5)

Table D–3

Discriminant Classification Percentages—BLUE Goods

	Execution	Proven	Communi-cation Index	Persuasion
Cannonical Correlation	.68	.59	.54	.56
Chi-Square Significance	.000	.000	.000	.014
Model 60% % Correctly Classified				
Poor Performing Ads	90.6% (115)	70.7% (99)	67.5% (77)	79.5% (62)
Good Performing Ads	77.2% (61)	81.4% (140)	78.2% (104)	63.9% (39)

Table D-3
(continued)

	Execution	Proven	Communi-cation Index	Persuasion
Holdout 40% % Correctly Classified:				
Poor Performing	82.9%	52.9%	64.4%	69.6%
Ads	(63)	(5)	(47)	(69)
Good Performing	52.3%	78.3%	66.0%	48.1%
Ads	(23)	(83)	(66)	(45)

Table D-4
Discriminant Classification Percentages—YELLOW Goods

	Execution	Proven	Communi-cation Index	Persuasion
Cannonical Correlation	.65	.56	.66	.66
Chi-Square Significance	.000	.000	.000	.000
Model 60% % Correctly Classified				
Poor Performing	75.7%	64.3%	78.0%	92.9%
Ads	(56)	(90)	(99)	(118)
Good Performing	86.1%	79.7%	85.1%	72.7%
Ads	(87)	(149)	(120)	(24)
Holdout 40% % Correctly Classified:				
Poor Performing	77.3%	51.0%	65.7%	86.8%
Ads	(34)	(50)	(69)	(92)
Good Performing	83.0%	78.0%	74.7%	57.1%
Ads	(44)	(85)	(59)	(12)

Table D–5
Discriminant Classification Percentages—
All Products Combined

	Execution	Proven	Communi-cation Index	Persuasion
Cannonical Correlation	.57	.47	.47	.48
Model 60%				
% Correctly Classified				
Poor Performing	78.2%	66.1%	71.8%	91.1%
Ads	(165)	(261)	(237)	(225)
Good Performing	73.8%	72.6%	72.3%	35.9%
Ads	(155)	(340)	(259)	(46)
Holdout 40%				
% Correctly Classified				
Poor Performing	76.1%	66.4%	65.9%	91.5%
Ads	(118)	(170)	(135)	(205)
Good Performing	67.6%	73.0%	67.1%	24.2%
Ads	(94)	(214)	(157)	(23)

The following ranges were used to define poor from good ads. The lowest 37% and highest 37% were predicted.

Execution Recall—lowest 37% = 0–5%
(range 0–100%) highest 37% = greater than 12%
not classified 25% = 6–11% execution recall

Proven Recall—lowest 37% = 0–9%
(range 0–100) highest 37% = greater than 16%
not classified = 10–15%

Communication Index—lowest 37% = 0–57%
(range 0–500%) highest 37% = greater than 94%
not classified 25% = 58–93%

Persuasion—lowest 37% = -65 to 0 persuasion
(range -65 to +62) highest 37% = 5–62 persuasion
not classified = 1–4 persuasion 25%
Mean for whole sample 2.5

References

Chapter 1

1. Historical accounts drawn from Carter, Alden, (1987) *Radio from Marconi to The Space Age,* New York: F. Watts.
2. Dygert, Warren B., (1985) *Radio as an Advertising Medium,* New York: Garland. Originally published New York: McGraw-Hill, 1939.

Chapter 2

1. *Radio Marketing Guide and Fact Book for Advertisers,* (1993), New York: Radio Advertising Bureau.
2. Schulberg, Bob, (1990), *Radio Advertising: The Authoritative Handbook,* Lincolnwood, IL: NTC Business Books.
3. Simmons Marketing Research Bureau (1990).
4. Radio Advertising Bureau, Inc., Success Story Library, 304 Park Avenue South, New York, NY, 10010.
5. Peter Gold, President, Gold & Ward Advertising, P.O. Box 846, Avon, CT, 06001.
6. *Radio Facts for Advertisers,* (1990), New York: Radio Advertising Bureau.
7. *Radio Marketing Guide and Fact Book for Advertisers,* (1992), New York: Radio Advertising Bureau.

8. Atwood, April, (1989), "Extending Imagery Research to Sounds: Is a Sound Also Worth a Thousand Words?" in T. Srull (ed.), *Advances in Consumer Research,* vol. 16, Ann Arbor, MI: Association for Consumer Research, pp. 587–94.

9. MacInnis, Deborah J. and Linda L. Price, (1987), "The Role of Imagery in Information Processing: Review and Extension," *Journal of Consumer Research,* vol. 13, pp. 473–91.

10. Miller, Darryl W. and Lawrence J. Marks, (1992), "Mental Imagery and Sound Effects in Radio Commercials," *Journal of Advertising,* vol. XXI, no. 4, December, pp. 83–93.

11. Bosley, Rhody, (1993), "Radio Study Tells Imagery Potential," *Advertising Supplement to Advertising Age,* September 6, p. R3.

12. Bone, Paula Fitzgerald and Pam Scholder Ellen, (1990), "The Effect of Imagery Processing and Imagery Content on Behavioral Intentions," in M. Goldberg, G. Gorn, and R. Pollay (eds.), *Advances in Consumer Research,* vol. 17, Ann Arbor, MI: Association for Consumer Research, pp. 449–54.

13. Blore, Chuck, CEO, The Chuck Blore Company, 1606 North Argyle, Hollywood, CA, 90028.

14. Barban, Arnold M., Steven M. Cristol and Frank J. Kopec (1988), *Essentials of Media Planning,* Lincolnwood, IL.: NTC Business Books.

15. Radio Case History (1983), "Molson Golden," Radio Advertising Bureau.

16. Marketing Successes, (1991), "Radio with a twist serves up sales success for beverage marketers," Radio Advertising Bureau.

17. Hill, Julie Skur, (1991), "Agencies Battle the 'Status Quo': Radio Spots Suffer at the Hand of Creatives," *Advertising Age,* September 9, pp. s-1–2.

18. Garfield, Bob, (1991), "In Need of Sound Advice: Radio Creative Overlooks the Power of Medium," *Advertising Age,* September 9, pp. s-1–2.

19. *The Interep Radio Store Success Story Book,* vol. III, The Interep Radio Store, 100 Park Avenue, New York, NY 10017.

Chapter 3

1. American Association of Advertising Agencies, "Advertising Campaign Report Newsletter," January 1979, 666 Third Ave, NY, NY 10017.

2. American Association of Advertising Agencies, "Advertising Campaign Report Newsletter," June 1980, 666 Third Ave, NY, NY 10017.
3. Sue Latremouille, Creative Manager, Radio Marketing Bureau, 146 Yorkville Avenue, Toronto, Ontario M5R1C2, Canada.

Chapter 4

1. Percy, Larry (1983), "A Review of the Effect of Specific Advertising Elements Upon Overall Communication Response" *Current Issues and Research in Advertising*, 77–118.
2. Gelb, Betsy D., Joe W. Hong and George M. Zinkhan (1985), Communications Effects of Specific Advertising Elements: An Update," *Current Issues and Research in Advertising*, 76–98.
3. Stewart, David W. and David H. Furse (1986), *Effective Television Advertising: A Study of 1000 Commercials*, Lexington, Mass: Lexington Books.
4. Ogilvy, David and Joel Raphaelson (1982), Research on Advertising Techniques that Work and Don't," *Harvard Business Review*, 60 (July-August), 14.
5. Burke Marketing Research, Inc. (1978), *The Effect of Environmental and Executional Variables on Overall Memorability*, Cincinnati: Burke Marketing Research, and McCollum/Spielman/ and Company, Inc. (1976), *The Influence of Executional Elements on Commercial Effectiveness*, Great Neck, N.Y.: McCollum/Spielman/and Company, Inc.
6. Caples, John (1983), *How to Make Your Advertising Make Money*, Englewood Cliffs, N.J.: Prentice Hall.
7. Book, Albert C., Norman D. Cary and Stanley I. Tannenbaum (1984), *The Radio and Television Commercial*, Chicago: Crain Books.
8. Sewall, Murphy A. and Dan Sarel (1986), "Characteristics of Radio Commercials and Their Recall Effectiveness", *Journal of Marketing*, 50(1) 52–60.
9. Petty, Richard, E., John T. Cacioppo and David Schumann (1983), "Central and Peripheral Routes to Advertising: Effectiveness: The Moderating Role of Involvement," *Journal of Consumer Research*, 10 (September) 135–146.
10. Vaughn, Richard (1986), "How Advertising Works: A Planning Model Revisited," *Journal of Advertising Research*, 26(2) 57–66.

11. Wells, William D. (1988), "Lectures and Dramas and Measurement Challenges," Paper presented at the Marketing Science Institute Conference, Wellesley, MA, June.
12. Rossiter, John R., Larry Percy and Robert J. Donovan (1990), "A Better Advertising Planning Grid," *Journal of Advertising Research,* 30 (5), 11–21.
13. Haley, Russell I. (1990), The ARF Copy Research Validity Project." Paper Presented at the Advertising Research Foundation's Copy Research Workshop, New York, July 11–12.
14. Ibid. Stewart and Furse.

Chapter 5

1. Gold & Ward Advertising, P.O. Box 846, Avon, CT 06001.
2. Joy Radio, 60 West 57th Street, New York, NY 10019.
3. *The Interep Radio Store Success Story Book,* vol. III, The Interep Radio Store, 100 Park Avenue, New York, NY 10017.
4. Southern California Broadcasters Association, 5670 Wilshire Boulevard, #910, Los Angeles, CA 90036.
5. Sacks/Fuller Advertising, 3435 Wilshire Boulevard, Los Angeles, CA 90010.
6. The Chuck Blore Company, 1606 North Argyle, Hollywood, CA, 90028.

Chapter 6

1. Southern California Broadcasters Association, 5670 Wilshire Boulevard, #910, Los Angeles, CA 90036.
2. Sacks/Fuller Advertising, 3435 Wilshire Boulevard, Los Angeles, CA 90010.
3. *The Interep Radio Store Success Story Book,* vol. III, The Interep Radio Store, 100 Park Avenue, New York, NY 10017.
4. L. A. Gear, 2850 Ocean Park Blvd., Santa Monica, CA 90405.
5. Sue Latremouille, Creative Manager, Radio Marketing Bureau, 146 Yorkville Avenue, Toronto, Ontario M5R 1C2, Canada.

Chapter 7

1. Sue Latremouille, Creative Manager, Radio Marketing Bureau, 146 Yorkville Avenue, Toronto, Ontario M5R 1C2, Canada.

2. Radio Advertising Bureau, Inc., 304 Park Avenue South, New York, NY 10010.
3. SmithKline Beecham, 100 Beecham Drive, Pittsburgh, PA 15205.
4. Radio Advertising Bureau, Inc., 304 Park Avenue South, New York, NY 10010.
5. Warner Wellcome, P.O. Box 647, Elk Grove, IL 60009–0647.
6. Sue Latremouille, Creative Manager, Radio Marketing Bureau, 146 Yorkville Avenue, Toronto, Ontario M5R 1C2, Canada.
7. Sue Latremouille, Creative Manager, Radio Marketing Bureau, 146 Yorkville Avenue, Toronto, Ontario M5R 1C2, Canada.

Chapter 8

1. Radio Advertising Bureau, Inc., 304 Park Avenue South, New York, NY 10010.
2. Freixenet USA, P.O. Box 1949, Sonoma, CA 95476.
3. Sue Latremouille, Creative Manager, Radio Marketing Bureau, 146 Yorkville Avenue, Toronto, Ontario M5R 1C2, Canada.
4. Pizza Hut of America, 400 Northridge Road, Suite 600, Atlanta, GA 30350.
5. The Interep Radio Store Success Story Book, vol. III, The Interep Radio Store, 100 Park Avenue, New York, NY 10017.
6. Radio Advertising Bureau, Inc., 304 Park Avenue South, New York, NY 10010.
7. Molson Breweries USA, 11911 Freedom Drive, Suite 1100, Reston, VA 22090–5609.
8. Radio Advertising Bureau, Inc., 304 Park Avenue South, New York, NY 10010.
9. Joy Radio, 60 West 57th Street, New York, NY 10019.

Chapter 9

1. New York Times, (December 28, 1993), The Media Business: Advertising column, Andrea Adelson.

Index

A

A&P Food Stores, 5
Advertising
  early, 3–4
  effectiveness of, 75–78
  revenue statistics, 9–10
Advertising agencies, views
  toward radio, 32–34
Advertising planning document
  advertising strategy, 40
  American Egg Board ad
    campaign, 48–53
  Blue Nun Wine ad
    campaign, 43–48
  case example summaries,
    58–60
  creative strategy and tactics,
    40–41
  media strategy and tactics,
    41–43
  Nutri-System ad campaign,
    53–58
  situation analysis, 38–39

Advertising profiles, 74–75
Advertising Research Founda-
  tion (ARF), 75–78
Advertising strategy
  American Egg Board ad
    campaign and, 50
  Blue Nun ad campaign and,
    44–45
  description of, 40
  Nutri-System ad campaign
    and, 54–55
Alpine Car Stereos, 109–10
Alwadish, David, 144
American Egg Board, 38
  advertising planning docu-
    ment for, 48–53
  media budget of, 42
  summary of, 59
American Express Co., 3
American Tobacco Co., 4
AT&T, 3, 4, 10
  "Feelings" advertising of, 26
  "Reach Out and Touch
    Someone," 26, 38, 41

Automobile advertising, Chevy
    Camaro, 25–26

            B

Bert Berdis and Co., 34, 131
Betty Crocker Frosting, media
    plan for, 28–29
Bleibtrau, Adam, 107
Blore, Chuck, 25–26, 97
Chuck Blore Co., 34, 97
Blue Nun wine, 39
    advertising planning docu-
        ment for, 43–48
    media budget of, 42
    summary of, 58–59
BLUE products
    comedy group reaches shop-
        ping masses, 123–24
    description of, 68–69, 74–75
    message structure elements,
        118–20
    message style elements,
        114–15
    method of analysis, 82–83
    mnemonics and sound ef-
        fects to sell throat loz-
        enges, 117–18
    mnemonics used to boost
        brand awareness, 121–22
    predictive performance,
        83–87
    presenter characteristics,
        122
    selling potatoes with related
        humor, 115, 117
    slice-of-life spots used to
        sell, 120–21
    structure of commericals,
        114

what works for, 114–26
Book, Albert C., 63
Brown, Garrett, 136
Burke Marketing Research,
    Inc., 62

            C

Campaign House, 132
Campbell-Mithun, 48
Canadian Association of Broad-
    casting (CAB), 5
Caples, John, 63
Cary, Norman D., 63
Cepacol/Cepastat Lozenges,
    117–18
Chevrolet
    Camaro advertising, 25–26
    "Heartbeat of America," 41
Chiat Day, 118
Coca-Cola Co., 10
Code of ethics, establishment
    of, 5
Cohen, Julie, 138
Columbia Broadcasting System
    (CBS), 4
    Radio Representatives, 8
Communication Index, 77, 78
Company goals and resources,
    analysis of, 39
Competition analysis
    Blue Nun ad campaign and,
        44
    description of, 39
    Nutri-System ad campaign
        and, 54
Conrad, Frank, 3
Cook, Dave, 118
Copy Research Validity Project,
    75–78

Cost-efficiency, 22–23
Craig, Jenny, 54
Creative strategy and tactics
    American Egg Board ad
        campaign and, 50–51
    Blue Nun ad campaign and,
        45–47
    description of, 40–41
    Nutri-System ad campaign
        and, 55–57
Creativity, 23–26
Customer analysis, 38–39

D

DDB Needham Worldwide, 66
Digital Audio Radio (DAR)
    Subcommittee, 145
Dixie Value Mall, 123–24
Domino's Pizza, 132–33
Donovan, Robert J., 66
Drive-time listening, 18

E

Elaboration Likelihood Model
    (ELM), 64, 67
Electronic Industries Associa-
    tion, 145
e.p.t. (Early Pregnancy Test),
    120–21

F

Foote, Cone, and Belding, 66
Ford, Henry, 3
Ford Motor Co., 10
Fragmentation, 32

Freixenet sparkling wine,
    131–32
Frequency medium, 23
Fromageries Bel, 137–39

G

Gillette, 3
Gimbels, 3
Gold, Peter, 91
Gold & Ward Advertising, 21,
    91
Golden, Joy, 91, 138
Grey Advertising, 48, 52

H

Haley, Russell, 76
Harris, Cole, Wilde Produc-
    tions, Inc., 110
"Heartbeat of America," 41
How to Make Your Advertising
    Make Money (Caples), 63
Humor
    selling boots with, 104–5
    selling cow cheeses with,
        137–39
    selling potatoes with, 115,
        117
Hungadunga, Hungadunga,
    Hungadunga,
        Hungadunga, & Mc-
        Cormick, 123
Hunt, Brian J., 133

I

"I Bought a Gun," 97
In-Band On Channel, 145

Information Resources Inc., 32
Interep Radio Store, 8, 9, 32
Ipana "Troubadours," 4

J

Joy Radio, 34, 91, 138

K

Katz Radio Group, 8, 9
KDKA, 3
Kmart Corp., 10
KNBC-TV, 97
Krogius, Kathleen, 94

L

L.A. Gear, 107–8
Lipton, Lynn, 138
Listerine, 121–22
Local spot advertising, 6
Lo Jack Stolen Vehicle Recovery System, 94–95
"Lucky Strike Radio Show," 4

M

McCollum/Spielman and Co., Inc., 62
McDonald's, 42
McElliott, Wright, Morrisson, & White, 118
McMillian, Thomas N., 120–21
Marconi, Guglielmo, 2
Marion Merrell Dow, 117
Market/competition analysis, 39

Marketing areas
cost-efficiency, 22–23
creativity, 23–26
frequency, 23
reach, 15–18
targetability, 18–22
Mass communication development of, 3
Maxwell House, 4
Media Concepts, 117
Media imperatives, 27
Media mix, radio in
Betty Crocker Frosting example, 28–29
description of, 26–27
Molson Golden Ale example, 29–32
Media strategy and tactics
American Egg Board ad campaign and, 51–52
Blue Nun ad campaign and, 47
description of, 41–43
Nutri-System ad campaign and, 57
Message recall. *See* Recall
Messages, approach for developing, 64
Message structure
for BLUE products, 118–20
coded commercial features used, 152
description of, 71–72
for RED products, 105–6
for WHITE products, 91–93
for YELLOW products, 133–36
Message style
for BLUE products, 114–15
coded commercial features used, 151–52

description of, 71
for RED products, 102–4
for WHITE products, 89–90
for YELLOW products,
128–31
Mnemonics
and sound effects to sell
throat lozenges, 117–18
used to boost brand awareness, 121–22
used to increase awareness,
131–32
Molson Breweries
media plan for Molson
Golden Ale, 29–32
slice-of-life radio spots for,
136
Myers, Jack, 34

N

National Association of Broad-
casters (NAB), 5
National Broadcasting Corp.
(NBC), 4
Blue Network, 4
Red Network, 4
National Radio Systems Com-
mittee, 145
National spot radio, 8
Network development, 4–5
Nutri/System in Canada
advertising planning docu-
ment for, 53–58
media budget of, 42–43
summary of, 59–60

O

Oglivy, David, 62

P

W.S. Palmer Co., 93–94
Pearl Drops, 40
Pepsico, 10
Percy, Larry, 66
Persuasion, 77–78
Petty, Richard, 64
Pizza Hut, 132–33
Political targeting, 21–22
Potato Marketing Board, 115,
117
Presenter category
for BLUE products, 122
coded commercial features
used, 152–53
description of, 72–73
for RED products, 108–9
for WHITE products, 95–96
for YELLOW products,
136–37
Procter & Gamble, 10
Product analysis
Blue Nun ad campaign and,
43–44
description of, 38
Nutri-System ad campaign
and, 53
Product color matrix (PCM)
background of, 65–67
BLUE products, 68–69, 74–75
correlations among mea-
sures, 155–56
discriminant classification
rates, 157–60
executional options, 70–75
message structure, 71–72
message style, 71
presenter category, 72–73
products represented in this
study, 69–70

[Product color matrix (PCM)]
RED products, 68, 74
tools versus toys, 67
WHITE products, 67–68, 74
YELLOW products, 69, 75
Product features, lifting of ban
against mentioning, 5
Promotional ability, 35

R

Raber, John W., 95
Radio
criticism of, 32–34
history of, 2–6
structure of, 6, 8–9
technological advances in,
144–46
Radio Advertising Bureau, 9
Radio Broadcast Data System
(RBDS), 144
RadioCard™, 144–45
"Radio Format Networks," 9
Radio Recall Research, Inc., 70
coded commercial features
used, 151–53
method and response mea-
sures, 147–50
Randazzo, Sydney, 131
Raphaelson, Joel, 62
Reach, 15–18
"Reach Out and Touch Someone," 26, 38, 41
Reaske, Peter, 136
Recall
creativity and, 24
execution, 77, 78
factors affecting, 61–62
measures of, 76–77

proven, 77, 78
Radio Recall Research, Inc.,
method and response mea-
sures, 147–50
RED products
demonstrating car stereos
with radio, 109–10
description of, 68, 74
message structure elements,
105–6
message style elements,
102–4
method of analysis, 82–83
predictive performance,
83–87
presenter characteristics,
108–9
selling boots with related
humor, 104–5
selling with testimonials,
107–8
structure of commericals,
101–2
what works for, 101–12
Rendall, Henry, 123–24
Repetition and consistency, selling with, 93–94
Research
radio advertising, 63
recent broadcast, 61–62
RisCassi & Davis, 90–91
Rossiter, John R., 66

S

Sacks, Cary, 104, 105
Sacks/Fuller Advertising, 94,
104
Sarel, Dan, 63

Sarnoff, David, 2, 4
Schieffelin & Co., 43
Schnieders, Frank, 138
Sears Roebuck & Co., 10
Serious radio, 90–91
Sewall, Murphy A., 63
Sex appeal, 32–33
"Showboat," 4
Situation analysis
    American Egg Board ad
        campaign and, 48–49
    Blue Nun ad campaign and,
        43–44
    description of, 38–39
    Nutri-System ad campaign
        and, 53–54
Slice-of-life spots, use of
    for BLUE products, 120–21
    for YELLOW products, 136
Smith, Murray, 58
Stiller and Meara, 46–47, 47
Sting, 132

T

Tannenbaum, Stanley I., 63
Targetability, 5–6, 18
    compared with other
        media, 20
    political, 21–22
    Western Union example,
        19, 21
Tauder Ford, Inc., 35
TBWA Advertising, 138
Technological advances, 144–46
Television, impact of, 6
Testimonials, selling with
    for RED products, 107–8
    for WHITE products, 94–95

Thieves Market, 104–5
J. Walter Thompson, 120, 121,
    122
Tidewater Oil, 3
Todd, Greg, 94
"Troubadours," 4
Truman, Richard, 132

U

Ultra-Brite toothpaste, 40
Unwired networks, 9

V

Veronis, Suhler & Associates,
    146

W

Warner-Lambert & Co., 10,
    120
Warner Wellcome, 120
WEAF, 3, 4
Weicker, Lowell, 21
Weight Watchers, 54
Western Union, 19, 21
Westinghouse, 2, 3
WFAN, 4
WHITE products
    description of, 67–68, 74
    message structure elements,
        91–93
    message style elements,
        89–90
    method of analysis, 82–83
    predictive performance,
        83–87

[WHITE products]
   presenter characteristics,
     95–96
   promoting serious issues, 97
   selling with repetition and
     consistency, 93–94
   selling with testimonials,
     94–95
   structure of commericals, 89
   success with serious radio,
     90–91
   what works for, 87–99
Winn, Ann, 136
Wired networks, 8
Wireless communication, development of, 2
WJZ, 4
WNBC, 4
Wood, Don, 26

Y

YELLOW products

Canadian beverage example, 132
description of, 69, 75
message structure elements,
   133–35
message style elements,
   128–31
method of analysis, 82–83
mnemonics used to increase
   awareness, 131–32
predictive performance,
   83–87
presenter characteristics,
   136–37
selling cow cheeses with
   related humor, 137–
   39
slice-of-life radio spot for
   Molson Breweries, 136
structure of commericals,
   127–28
use of catchy jingle for
   Pizza Hut, 132–33
what works for, 128–41

About the Authors

Marc G. Weinberger is professor of marketing at the University of Massachusetts at Amherst. He received his Ph.D. and taught at Arizona State University. Dr. Weinberger has conducted research and written extensively about advertising issues. His work has explored the use of humor and other message devices in magazines, television, and radio advertising. He is currently serving on the editorial boards of several major advertising and marketing journals.

Leland Campbell is assistant professor of marketing at Bentley College. He received his Ph.D. from the University of Massachusetts at Amherst. His research has focused on consumer response to sales promotions and advertising, and currently he is investigating the impact of cause-related marketing on consumer attitudes. Professor Campbell is profiled in *Who's Who in Advertising*.

Beth Brody is a writer for many major American corporations in the advertising and financial industries. Ms. Brody spent several years at The Interep Radio Store, where she wrote the firm's annual volume of radio success stories. She began her career as an editor for leading technical magazines.